INUIT
GLIMPSES OF AN ARCTIC PAST

INUIT

GLIMPSES OF AN ARCTIC PAST

DAVID MORRISON
and
GEORGES-HÉBERT GERMAIN

Illustrations by
FRÉDÉRIC BACK

CANADIAN MUSEUM OF CIVILIZATION

CANADIAN MUSEUM   MUSÉE CANADIEN
OF CIVILIZATION   DES CIVILISATIONS

PUBLISHER: Jean-François Blanchette
PROJECT ORIGINATOR AND DIRECTOR: André Bastien
PRODUCTION COORDINATOR: Cécile Masse
INUIT READER AND CONTENT EDITOR: Edna Elias
MANAGING EDITOR: Cathrine Wanczycki
TEXT EDITOR: Marcia Rodriguez
FICTION TRANSLATOR: Käthe Roth
FICTION EDITOR: Margaret Campbell
DESIGN: France Lafond

Legal deposit fourth quarter, 1995
ISBN: 0-660-14038-1

This work is translated and adapted from
INUIT, les Peuples du Froid, published by
Éditions Libre Expression, 1995.
ISBN: 2-89111-642-9

Canadian Cataloguing in Publication Data
Morrison, David A., 1951—
Inuit: glimpses of an Arctic past
Includes bibliographical references.
ISBN: 0-660-14038-1
1. Inuit - Social life and customs.
2. Arctic peoples - Social life and customs.
I. Germain, Georges-Hébert, 1944 — , II. Back, Frédéric,
III. Canadian Museum of Civilization. IV. Title

E99.E7M67 1995   390'.089'971   C95-940962-9

CONTENTS

Once all the men at Kamigluk went hunting for caribou
and only the women were left. The men urged them not
to fish from the edge of the ice, but the women did so
just the same. Suddenly the ice went adrift and they
dared not jump ashore; there was only one who took
the risk, and she was saved. All the others went
out to sea and were lost. So pitiful were their
cries and screams out on the drifting ice
that from a distance it sounded like the
howls of terrified foxes.
    But when the men came home they
sorrowed so deeply over the loss of their
women that they built cairns up on the
shore, just as many cairns as there were
women lost. They did this because they
wanted the souls of the drowned women
to be on dry land not out in
the wet sea.

FOREWORD

This book is about the Inuit, in particular the Copper Inuit of the Central Canadian Artic. It is written in the past tense, not because the Inuit are a people of the past, but simply because the story is set in the year 1909-10. That year marked something of a turning point for the Copper Inuit. Previously they had been free to live their own lives, outside the orbit of Western civilization and its commerce. They had been visited by a few European explorers, representing either the British Royal Navy or the Hudson's Bay Company, but to little obvious effect. After 1910 they were never without outside visitors, visitors who came to stay.

First appeared the scientific explorers of the Stefánsson-Anderson and Canadian Arctic expeditions, along with schooner-based fur traders such as Joseph Bernard and Christian Klengenberg. The three main pillars of frontier Canadian society arrived in 1916: the RCMP (then still called the Royal Northwest Mounted Police), the Hudson's Bay Company (which opened its first permanent post that year), and an Anglican mission. Having established its sovereignty, the Canadian government belatedly and somewhat reluctantly assumed responsibility for the people and their welfare, introducing compulsory schooling, medical services, and family allowance cheques. The 1950s and 1960s witnessed the great change from life on the land to life in the new, government-built towns. There are now five settlements in the Copper Inuit area: Holman, Coppermine, Cambridge Bay, Bay Chimo, and Bathurst Inlet.

Despite sometimes severe hardship, the Copper Inuit have survived and adapted. Indeed, they now number about three times as many people as they did in 1910 (about 2,500), and enjoy considerable self-government through two land-claim agreements, the Nunavut and Inuvialuit agreements. But their life and culture as described here survive only in explorers' accounts, museum archives, and in the early childhood memories of the very oldest Copper Inuit elders.

CHAPTER 1

A YOUNG GIRL FROM NOAHOGNIR

When Kahina went outside for a breath of fresh air, the sun was just climbing above the horizon. The sea ice stretched around her as far as she could see like a flat white plain. The grooves and ripples that the restless wind had etched in the surface glittered, sharp-edged, as the rays touched them.

Between 1914 and 1916 the Copper Inuit were visited by the Canadian Arctic Expedition. A New Zealander — Diamond Jenness — was the expedition's anthropologist, while G.H. Wilkins, who took this photograph, was the official photographer.

Behind her, the snowhouses huddled together, little round, plump bumps turning pink in the low sun. Cries and laughter from the women and children inside floated in the air.

Kahina lifted her face to the light. She had spent the winter inside, waiting for the end of the long night. The dark months had passed slowly this year. She had helped her mother with all the usual tasks — butchering the seals that the men brought back from the hunt, repairing the clothes, tending the lamp — and she had laughed with her friends and dreamed about the future, but nothing had helped to speed the hours.

And then a tantalizing light had appeared on the horizon, making a little day that began and ended in the wink of an eye. It had been so short, with dawn and dusk so close together, that it might have been just a passing fancy. But it had lifted spirits, and none more than Kahina's, for she had a special reason to look forward to the returning sun.

Akuluk had managed to surprise her, though. She hadn't expected him so soon. No one travelled alone through the winter darkness: it was too risky. But he had done it, and everyone was full of admiration. The whole village was talking about how bold and resourceful he was.

She turned to look at the shadow stretching behind her, so long and narrow that it could surely slip into one of the ice cracks to hide. When she was small, she and her friends had loved to play with their shadows!

But the time for games would soon be over. In a few days, she would be leaving with Akuluk to live in Kanghiryuak, on the other side of the sea. In her heart was a great strange, anxious joy when she thought about this. She was eager to be alone with him, and she was confident she could be a good wife. She knew how to handle the seals and the caribou he would catch, how to turn the skins into clothing for him, how to take care of the lamp. And she knew what a man wants when he approaches a woman. But would Akuluk be as gentle with her as her cousin Punniq had been? And would she be welcomed at Kanghiryuak? She knew she had relatives in Akuluk's family, so she wouldn't be a total stranger, but did they like to laugh the way she did? Did the children play with their shadows when the sun came back? Did they all sleep together, wrapped in big, soft caribou skins? It was said that winter nights in Kanghiryuak were even longer and darker than they were in Noahognir and the winds harsher, and that there were many huge and very ferocious bears....

Kila and Kanneyuq, adopted sisters of Diamond Jenness, already wear very decorative, adult-style clothing despite their youth. Kanneyuq died of spinal tuberculosis in 1931, about fifteen years after this photograph was taken.

To compensate Kahina's parents for the loss of their daughter, Akuluk would offer them a gift, something useful and beautiful that he had found in the foreign land where he had been travelling. He had brought back all sorts of things, piled onto the magnificent sled he had made himself. Where he had been,

10

there were real trees, he told them, some of them taller than a man. There was no copper, but there was iron, the most precious and useful material in the world. In fact, Kahina's mother was hoping that Akuluk's gift would be an iron cooking pot. In a few days, she would make a big party in their honour. There would be laughter, games, dancing, and plenty of food. The next day, long before the new sun had risen, Akuluk would pack his sled, Kahina would climb on, and she would be on her way to her new life.

Daydreaming, Kahina turned back toward the snowhouses. Even though she loved it here, she wouldn't miss it for long. In fact, her father had told her, just yesterday, that they would have to move again soon. The seals were getting scarcer; the men and dogs had searched the sea ice for hours but had found almost nothing, just abandoned breathing holes already being frozen over by new ice. It would be the third time this winter that they had had to load everything onto sleds and set off for new hunting grounds.

She had met Akuluk almost a year ago, just before they left the sea ice to spend the summer on the land. One fine evening, he had arrived at Noahognir to stay for a few days. Kahina was fascinated by him right away. He didn't talk much, but every time he opened his mouth, everyone listened, even the elders. Tall and handsome, with a very round, sunburned face, he seemed very sure of himself. Although he was probably over twenty, he didn't have a woman with him. Kahina and her friends amused themselves imagining all sorts of things: that his wife was pregnant or had a newborn and couldn't travel, that she had died or been abducted, or that she had run away with someone else. When he left, a few days later, they hadn't found out much more about him.

During that first stay, Akuluk had barely spoken to Kahina. She told herself that she was still too young to interest him. She was wrong. He had gone out of his way to come and see her again. He must have noticed that she had changed quite a bit. On his first visit, she had had just a few tattoos on her hands and wrists; by the time he returned, she had them on her forehead and cheeks, around her eyes, even near her lips, which were still sore from the needle.

Since then, Akuluk had been to Akilinik, very far away. He had many stories to tell about his long trip. He had passed through the country of the Netsilik, a strange, taciturn people who kept their thoughts to themselves. He had seen the *qablunaq*, the pale people who looked like — but weren't — men; he had even traded with them. Although he spoke for hours and hours, everyone listened attentively and respectfully.

While in Noahignir, Akuluk stayed with Kahina's family, sleeping in the big common bed. The first night, Kahina's father assigned him a place at the very back, against the snow wall. Every day, Akuluk went hunting with Kahina's father and her brother, Naneoroak, who would marry Kahina's best friend, Koptana, as soon as he had become an accomplished hunter. Akuluk proved to be a good hunter and a pleasant companion. Even though everyone knew why he was there, no one talked about it. But Kahina's friends and family — first Koptana, then Naneoroak, then even her father and mother — had started exchanging smiles and sidelong glances and arranging for her and Akuluk to be alone together as much as possible.

Tonight or tomorrow night, Kahina's parents would reshuffle the sleeping platform and let Akuluk spend the night lying beside their daughter. The children would fall sleep very quickly, as they always did. No doubt, the adults too would lie still and quiet, pretending that they were dreaming.

THE PEOPLE OF THE COLD

An ancient Inuit story tells of a girl, Kannakapfaluk (sometimes called Sedna or Niviarsiang, or any of a dozen other names), who was married to a dog as a punishment for her stubborn refusal to choose a suitor. Her new husband took her to his island, where they had many puppies. For revenge, one day Kannakapfaluk put the children in her boots and set them out to sea. One boot landed not far away, and the children (or puppies) in it became the ancestors of the Indians. They at least were said to look human, although they had their father's heart. The other boot drifted across the ocean, and the puppies in it became the ancestors of the *qablunaq*, the white men, who one day returned to the Arctic in their sailing ships. With their hairy bodies and bearded faces (*qablunaq* means "heavy eyebrows"), they resembled their dog-father even in outward appearance.

This necklace of wolf foot bones was worn on the front of a woman's coat. Such objects were often considered to have magical properties, embuing the wearer with some of the qualities of the animal represented.

The Inuit are the aboriginal inhabitants of about half of the world's Arctic, from Bering Strait to the eastern coast of Greenland, a straight-line distance of over 6,000 kilometres. Like Kannakapfaluk (who went on to become the Mother of All Sea Mammals and a spirit of great power), they have many different names for themselves — Inupiat in Alaska, Inuvialuit in the Mackenzie Delta area, Inuit in the rest of Arctic Canada and Greenland — all terms meaning "people" or "real people." Until recently, outsiders usually called them Eskimo, a word of Algonquin Indian origin apparently meaning "eaters of raw meat." Because this book focuses on the Central Arctic, the Canadian term "Inuit" is used throughout.

Despite the immensity of their homeland and the number of different terms they have for themselves, the Inuit are everywhere remarkably uniform as a people. All speak dialects of the same language, commonly called Inuktitut in Canada but going by a number of regional names as well. As their traditional storytellers knew, they are genetically distinct from the Indians living to the south of them, although not as different as they are from Europeans, or Africans. Their closest relations are the people of northeastern Asia, the Chukchi and the Koryak of Siberia, for example, and they belong to the same great family of humankind as the Chinese and the Koreans.

The popular cartoon image of the Inuit as chubby and round is due largely to the effects of heavy winter clothing. In traditional times, few Inuit were fat, and the men, especially, tended to be spare and well-muscled. Their height often fell a little below the average for humanity as a whole, but not greatly so, typically between about 160 and 165 centimetres for men. Average height seems to have varied geographically, with the tallest Inuit living in Alaska and around the mouth of the Mackenzie River, and the shortest in the eastern Arctic. Nutrition may be an important factor here, for modern Inuit teenagers are usually taller than their parents, and much taller than their grandparents.

Father Guy Marie-Rousselière lived from 1938 until his death in 1994 among the peoples of Northern Canada. In the early 1960s he participated in a film project among the Netsilik Inuit, the immediate eastern neighbours of the Copper Inuit. His many photographs from that project provide a faithful colour witness to traditional life in the Central Arctic.

Drying rack

Ivory comb

Pendant made from the lower jaw and teeth of a caribou

Tattooing was very painful. Some Inuit believed that women who failed to undergo the process (which might take several years to complete) went with other wrong-doers to an especially miserable place after death.

Double snowhouse

The dome of a snowhouse is so strong that an adult can quite safely stand on the roof

While legs are short, torsos tend to be relatively long, so that most Inuit have a comparatively tall sitting height. Hands and feet are usually small. The hair on the head is black, coarse, and straight, while facial and body hair are scanty. Skin colour is clear and quite pale except where it is exposed to the sun, when it can tan as dark as leather. Although babies are usually born with the famous "Mongolian blue spot" at the base of the spine, this spot fades in childhood.

None of these traits is unique, at least as far as Northeast Asian populations are concerned. There are other physical characteristics, however, that taken together mark the Inuit as a distinctive people. Dark, almond-shaped eyes, a small, almost bridgeless nose, a very strong jaw, high cheekbones, and round cheeks: this is the typical Inuit face. In the ABO blood group system they show a much lower frequency of type B than in Siberia, although higher than among North American Indians (where it is practically non-existent), while frequencies of type A are higher than among either of their neighbours — among the highest in the world, in fact.

The Inuit seem to have a higher metabolic rate than most other people. Their hands work better in extreme cold, and they have excellent circulatory systems. Much of this is probably acquired from a lifetime of exposure to cold, to untangling wet fish nets at -30° C, or waiting motionless at a seal's breathing hole through any weather. But the myth that the Inuit do not feel the cold is untrue. They simply realize that it is futile to complain.

It has often been suggested that at least some of the physical characteristics of the Inuit (and their Siberian relatives) represent a genetically based adaptation to a very cold climate. The argument is attractive. A flat face and small extremities are easier to keep warm. An epicanthic fold helps protect the eye not only from freezing, but also from the intense sunlight of spring, which can cause snow blindness. The relative lack of facial hair can also be attributed to adaptation. Although most people consider a beard a facial blanket of sorts, in intense cold it collects ice condensed from the breath (imagine every picture of a white Arctic explorer you have ever seen), and is more of a liability than an asset. Even the powerful jaw may be an adaptation to a very tough diet, which could regularly include items such as raw, frozen meat or walrus hide.

But whatever physical adaptations the Inuit have made, they are comparatively minor. Differences between human groups are nowhere profound, and the great key to Inuit success in the Arctic has not been their physiology, but their culture. The Inuit live in probably the most difficult environment on earth. They have survived because of their intelligence, resourcefulness, and spirit of cooperation, and above all because they know what to do in order to thrive. This is something they have learned from their parents and grandparents, from the accumulated knowledge of thousands of years. So it is with all human groups; we all stand on the shoulders of our ancestors. In the Arctic, the debt seems more obvious.

WOMEN'S CLOTHING

One of the keys to Inuit survival has been the development of the warmest, lightest clothing in the world. Not only did it provide protection from the elements, but it also made a statement about the wearer's taste and the accomplishments of the seamstress who made it. Clothing was never merely practical.

The Inuit applied the principle of layering in their winter clothing. Air trapped between layers of caribou hide helped keep the wearer warm under almost any conditions.

Trousers

Worn with the hair side against the skin

Worn with the hair side against the skin

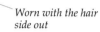
Worn with the hair side out

From birth, a newborn passed its earliest days almost naked beneath its mother's coat, skin-to-skin against her back. Designed to accommodate a baby, the coat was roomy in the back where the child rested, held by a belt tied around the mother's waist. The front was cut large as well, so that the infant could be swung around to the breast without being exposed to the frigid outside air. And the hood was large enough for both mother and child, one face peeking out behind the other.

In cold weather, women put on an inner and outer coat, both cut to a similar pattern. The inner garment was worn with the hair side next to the skin, while the outer coat was worn hair-side-out. Pockets of air trapped between the layers of fur and hide make this arrangement unsurpassed for warmth; as a result, this design principle is repeated over and over. Coats were always pullover style, without a front flap or vent through which heat could be lost.

The design of women's coats varied from area to area according to different regional tastes. Among the Copper Inuit (Kahina's group), the style was quite distinctive. Shoulders were greatly enlarged and pointed,

giving a characteristic samurai-like profile, while the bottom edge of the garment was cut short at the waist. With a narrow tail behind and a smaller strip or triangle often sewn to the middle of the front bottom edge as well, this style seems to be an abbreviated form of the tailed woman's coat common to most of the Central and Eastern Arctic.

Women dressed in two pairs of short, above-the-knee trousers underneath the coat in winter. Again, the inner pair was worn hair-side-in, the outer pair hair-side-out. Below this came voluminous caribou-hide stockings or boots. They enclosed the foot, and after fitting snugly at the ankles, became very baggy at the knee, fitting over the bottom of the trousers. They then encased the outer thigh, and were tied to the belt on the outside of the hips, rather like a pair of modern hip-waders. As might be expected, both an inner and an outer pair were used. Finally, several layers of ankle-high socks or slippers covered the feet, followed by a pair of sealskin outer shoes. Mittens were also part of winter attire, but never a cap, since the hood kept the head warm enough.

Summer called for no special clothing styles. As temperatures

Copper Inuit woman's parka. Women took a great deal of pleasure in making and owning well-made, intricately decorated clothing. An elegant coat like this would have been especially appropriate on festive occasions such as drum dances.

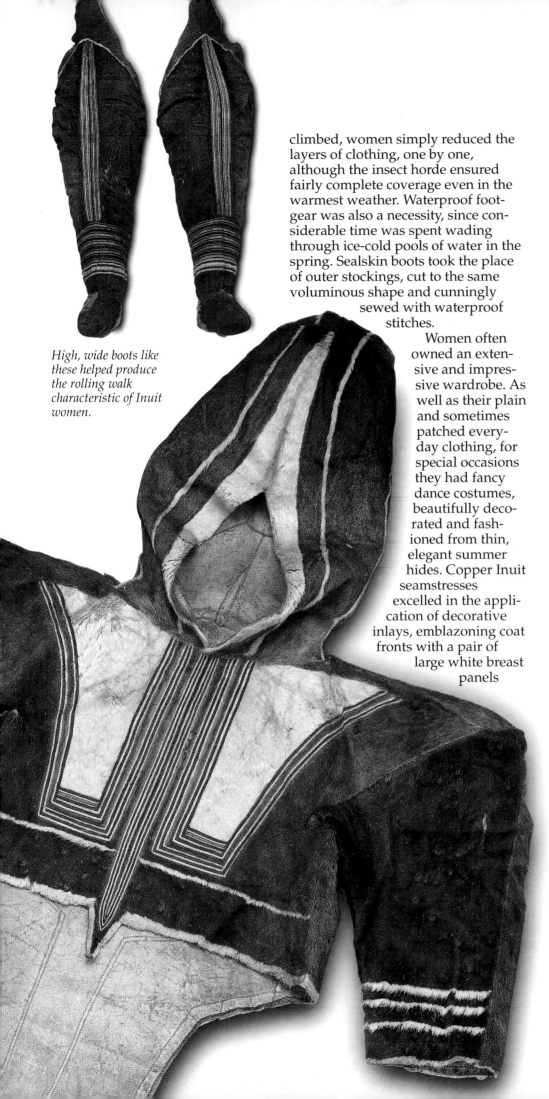

High, wide boots like these helped produce the rolling walk characteristic of Inuit women.

climbed, women simply reduced the layers of clothing, one by one, although the insect horde ensured fairly complete coverage even in the warmest weather. Waterproof footgear was also a necessity, since considerable time was spent wading through ice-cold pools of water in the spring. Sealskin boots took the place of outer stockings, cut to the same voluminous shape and cunningly sewed with waterproof stitches.

Women often owned an extensive and impressive wardrobe. As well as their plain and sometimes patched everyday clothing, for special occasions they had fancy dance costumes, beautifully decorated and fashioned from thin, elegant summer hides. Copper Inuit seamstresses excelled in the application of decorative inlays, emblazoning coat fronts with a pair of large white breast panels made from inserts of white fur. White inserts also highlighted both the front and back coat tails, and inlaid white bands usually encircled the upper arms. Trousers too had an inset triangle in the front, and de-haired strips of caribou hide dyed red sewn in as accents. Great pride was taken in the quality of workmanship. A woman would never attend a drum dance wearing anything but her best.

Some women had more taste and ambition than others, of course, and no Inuit seamstress was entirely bound by tradition. It was not unusual to copy or adapt designs seen elsewhere, which may account for the general thematic similarity in clothing styles over wide areas, however much the surface details might differ.

Clothing was decorated in other ways too. Women frequently adorned themselves with what we might call fashion accessories: a lemming-skin pendant buttoned on the back of the coat, or fox-bone necklaces. They were usually worn as *atagtat*, or amulets, objects imbued with religious or magical significance. Every mother carrying a baby sewed one or more amulets to her coat so that her child would be a skilful hunter or efficient housewife. Wolf bones, for instance, made men clever and enduring hunters, the skin from a great northern diver gave long life, and an ermine skin could make one agile and fleet of foot. The object should come from an animal killed by a close relative, an uncle or grandfather, for example. These *atagtat* would be transferred to the child's clothing when he or she started to walk.

Women's tattoos, on the other hand, seem to have been purely decorative. Typically restricted to visible areas such as the face, hands, and arms, they followed stereotyped geometric patterns, which varied only a little according to the whim of the individual. Tattooing was usually done with a copper sewing needle and sinew thread that had been rubbed with lamp soot. The thread was pulled beneath the skin, leaving the soot behind. Because of the pain involved, most sessions were short, and it could take years before the process was finished.

THE SEAMSTRESS

Sewing an Arctic wardrobe was a complicated, time-consuming job that demanded not only the mechanical skill necessary to cut out patterns and sew seams, but also considerable knowledge about the physical properties of different kinds of animal skin. Of all the examples of Inuit ingenuity, proper clothing was perhaps the most important.

Antler handle

Raw copper blade

An ulu or crescent-shaped knife was a woman's most important tool.

Providing the insulation between tender organism and brutal environment, good clothing was the one thing that more than any other made life possible in the Arctic for a naked and essentially tropical animal. Charged with symbolism and weighted with taboo, the working of animal hides was a highly refined technology, and a task that naturally fell to the women.

The Copper Inuit woman always kept her sewing kit close at hand, sometimes in a small lidded sewing basket woven from grass or willow twigs. The needlecase, almost an emblem of femininity, consisted of a bone tube bleached white by the sun, polished by years of handling, and incised with geometric designs reminiscent of women's tattooing. Within the tube ran a strip of hide, through which were threaded the precious copper sewing needles. Hide or bone thimbles were attached on the outside, sometimes suspended from elaborately decorated thimble holders.

Another invaluable tool was the semi-lunar knife, the *ulu*. Practically as much a part of a woman as her hands, it was used for almost as many purposes: cutting out patterns, cutting meat, eating, splitting sinews, de-hairing a hide. Losing an ulu was considered bad luck, but it could not have happened very often that a woman seriously misplaced something so constantly in use.

With her ulu, needles, awls, and various hide scrapers, the Inuit seamstress spent her days working skins and making clothes. And not only clothes, but spring and summer tents, dog harnesses, kayak covers, sealskin sacks and bags — in short, almost everything made of hide, fur, or skin. From marriage to death, a woman was

Whenever possible most clothing was made from caribou hide, since it is light, supple, and very warm. Unfortunately, it easily sheds its hair.

A seamstress uses her ulu to cut out a pattern from caribou hide.

Sealskin often had to be softened by chewing before it could be sewn into clothing.

moved from the land out onto the sea ice, usually sometime in December. From then until the sun returned in late January, it was forbidden to sew new garments (although old ones could be repaired). Otherwise the consequences could be disastrous, for the spirits would be offended and the whole village might be destroyed. Unfortunately, by late autumn the daylight hours are few in number at Arctic latitudes, and sewing by lamplight added eye strain to the seamstresses already heavy load.

Whenever possible, most clothing was made from caribou hide. With its hollow hairs, it is perhaps the warmest natural material known, supple and very light. Caribou also supplied an excellent sewing thread made from sinews in the back muscles. These sinews were carefully separated out from the meat, dried, then twisted together to make a nearly unbreakable thread.

The Copper Inuit did not tan skins, nor alter them chemically. Instead, they first scraped them clean of fat, then laid them out to dry in the sun, fur-side to the ground. Holes were patched, blood stains washed with dry snow, and the entire inside scraped using a sharp, copper-bladed scraper to soften it and clean off the inner membrane, or epidermis. To soften the hide further, it was wetted, folded up, laid aside for a few hours, and scraped again with a dull scraper made of bone. The hair could then be shaved off if desired, but for the most part it was left on for warmth.

The quality of caribou hide changes with the seasons. Hides are at their prime in late summer and early autumn — August through September. Earlier in the season they are nearly useless, since animals are shedding their winter coats and the hair comes out in handfuls. Spring hides too are often full of holes from escaping larval parasites. The Copper Inuit preferred to make most of their clothing from hides taken in August. Comparatively light and short-haired, such hides were considered elegant and stylish. At the same time, they were not particularly warm, and men's heavy winter coats and trousers were usually made instead

responsible for keeping her husband and children clothed, using all the skills taught by her mother, which she in turn would pass on to her daughter.

Something of the diligence with which this most feminine of arts was practised is dramatically illustrated by a recent find from the West Greenland coast, the body of a middle-aged Inuit woman who lived about five hundred years ago, mummified in the dry, frigid air of the small burial cave where she was found. She evidently died blind and in considerable pain from a malignant facial tumour, yet cut marks on her left thumbnail show how she continued to work splitting sinews for thread up until a few days or hours of her death.

Late autumn was the busiest time of year for the Inuit seamstress. The winter clothing had to be ready by the time of winter darkness, when people

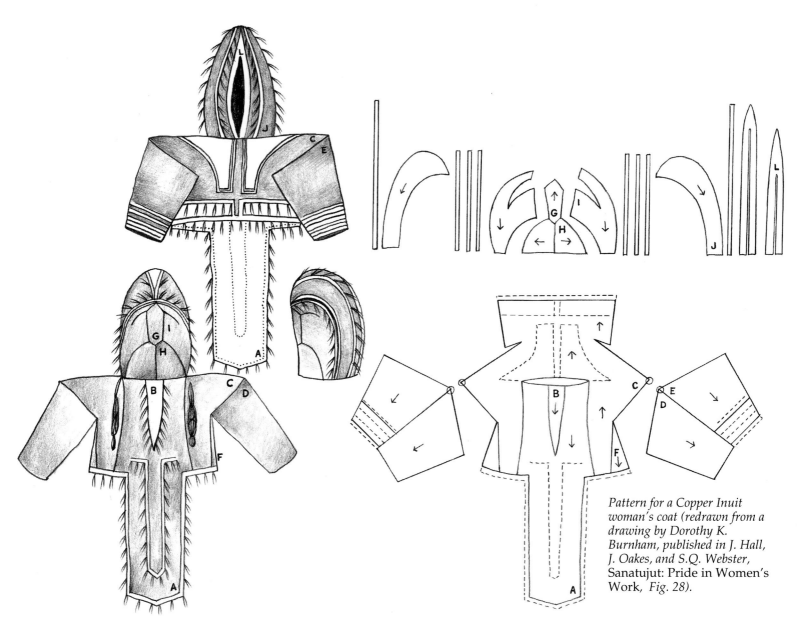

Pattern for a Copper Inuit woman's coat (redrawn from a drawing by Dorothy K. Burnham, published in J. Hall, J. Oakes, and S.Q. Webster, Sanatujut: Pride in Women's Work, *Fig. 28).*

from thicker September hides. Early winter hides are heavier yet, and were used mainly for bedding, footwear, diapers, and sometimes mittens. The soft skin from very young animals was used for children's clothing.

Caribou are rare or unobtainable in a few areas of the Arctic, for instance on the islands in Bering Strait, or on the Belcher Islands in the middle of Hudson Bay. Although every effort was made to obtain the necessary hides by trade, it often happened that there was a gap between supply and demand. Extraordinary ingenuity was then required to find substitutes. The people of the Belchers, for instance, specialized in winter clothing made of eider duck skin, complete with feathers. These garments were nearly as warm and light as caribou, but very fragile and extremely difficult to sew.

On the west coast of Victoria Island and in a few other areas where bears were particularly abundant, men sometimes wore trousers made from polar bear skin. They were warm and fairly light, but their stiffness made them somewhat uncomfortable to wear. Nonetheless, they had a certain cachet, marking their wearer as someone who had killed a polar bear. Polar bear hide being very water-resistant, it was also used for mittens, as a foot pad for standing on while seal hunting, or for applying the coat of ice on the bottom of sled runners.

Musk-ox hide was too shaggy and heavy for any but rough purposes — as a mattress for instance, or to cushion the load on a sled. Only rarely or in an emergency was it used to make a very heavy and not very serviceable coat.

The blade of this ulu was made from an English butcher knife.

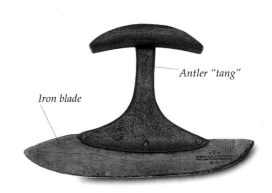

Antler "tang"

Iron blade

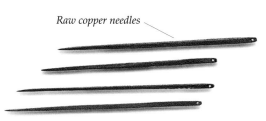

Handle, or "pull"

Leather strip

Thimble-holder

Thimble

Copper Inuit needlecases consisted of a decorated bone tube, through which was run a strip of leather. The needles were carried stuck into the leather. Although these tools would have been made for a woman by her husband, they were considered her personal property.

Raw copper needles

These sewing needles are about 8 centimetres long.

The Inuit wasted nothing, and every kind of skin was put to some use. Children's clothing, bags, socks, and trimmings for boots and mittens were fashioned from soft lemming or ground squirrel skins. Fox skins were sometimes considered stylish for an outer coat. Wolf, dog, and wolverine fur functioned as trim, particularly on coat hoods as they shed frost. Rabbit skins, too easily torn for most purposes, were made into diapers, towels, or socks. Ptarmigan skins with feathers attached served as towels, and loon skins as whisks for beating off summer mosquitoes. Feet skins from swans, geese, and ducks were sewn into tinder bags. Even fish skins could be turned into tool bags.

But only sealskin approached the importance of caribou. Light and very strong, it wears well and offers the major advantage that it can be made waterproof. Unfortunately, it is not especially warm, and so was used mainly in making summer clothing — waterproof boots and rain jackets — as well as kayak and tent coverings, and various bags and buckets.

The preparation of sealskins followed much the same lines as for caribou. The skin was cleaned and the epidermis on the inside removed. After it had been washed vigorously with water and snow and pegged out to dry, it was softened by scraping,

often augmented by chewing. Seal hides are particularly stiff and required a lot of manual (or dental) softening. For many purposes the hair was removed by soaking in warm water, then scraping with a knife. Hides were also steeped in urine to make them more waterproof.

Although sometimes used for boot soles, the skins of large bearded seals were too heavy for most clothing, yet made exceptionally strong rope, handy for dog harnesses, for lashing sleds together, and for similar heavy tasks. In many areas of the Arctic, bearded seal, beluga, or walrus hides were used for boat covers. The intestines of walrus and whales were also used for tent or house windows, and to make the waterproof body suit worn by sea kayakers.

The Inuit had to be very careful to avoid getting their clothing wet. Because the hides were not chemically tanned, they became stiff when they dried out again. In winter, outer garments were removed in the entrance passage rather than brought into the house. Any clothing will collect body moisture, which in the Arctic can freeze into a kind of hoar frost trapped between the various layers or even, in the case of skin clothing, within the hair follicles themselves. If not dealt with, this frost and moisture will build up from day to day, eventually making clothes unusable, as many European Arctic explorers found to their cost. The Inuit allowed their clothes to freeze hard in the entrance tunnel, then beat out the frost using a special wooden or antler paddle. Clothes could then be brought indoors and placed on a drying rack suspended over the lamp.

It was sometimes impossible to keep clothes dry, particularly boots during the summer. Inevitably, the next day they would be rock-hard. The only practical way to soften them was by chewing; hence, the stereotyped picture of the Inuit woman chewing her husband's boots. The image is a true one, and the work involved was long and tedious. By the time a woman reached old age, her teeth were often worn flat to the gum line by countless hours of hide chewing.

Copper blade and tang

Copper blade

This ulu, with a "tang-less" handle, comes from an 800-year old archaeological site in the Copper Inuit region.

UNDER THE GREAT BEAR

For most of humanity the Arctic is literally the end of the world.
It takes its name, fittingly, from the Greek word for bear, *arktos*,
for this is the land under the constellation of the Great Bear.

The Arctic may be defined in several ways. One of them is astronomical, for the declination of the earth as it revolves about the sun results in extreme differences between the length of night and day at different seasons of the year. The Arctic Circle (66°30' N) is the lowest latitude at which there is at least one twenty-four-hour period when the sun neither rises above the horizon in winter, nor sets below it in summer. Near the northern limit of the Copper Inuit, at the 70th parallel, the polar night is nearly two months long, and it continues to lengthen the farther north one goes. At Alert, on the northern end of Ellesmere Island, it lasts four months.

A LAND WITHOUT TREES

The Arctic may also be defined by the absence of trees owing to cold. Tree growth is largely dependent on summer temperature, and the northern limit of trees generally follows the July 10°C isotherm, in a line that zigzags through the mountains of northern Alaska, nearly reaches the sea at the mouth of the Mackenzie River, and then plunges southeast deep into the heart of the continent, reaching Hudson Bay at about the latitude of Churchill, Manitoba. Much of far northern Quebec is beyond the limit of trees, as is the Labrador coast. Of the two definitions, this is the more satisfactory, for the astronomical definition would exclude the southern portion of two such "arctic" lands as Baffin Island and Greenland.

The Arctic is not the coldest place in the world in absolute terms. The Subarctic immediately to the south has colder winters, since the Arctic Ocean even under its mantle of ice exerts a moderating effect. Winter temperatures are only about 10° C colder than they are on the northern Canadian prairies. February is the coldest month, with average temperatures in much of the Arctic fluctuating between a daily high of about -25° C and a daily low of about -35° C. What distinguishes the Arctic climate is not absolute cold but the

Although they are much smaller than they were in the Ice Age, Arctic glaciers are always active. In certain areas of Greenland they are as much as 3,000 metres thick.

length of the winter and the coolness of the summer. In the Central Arctic, the sea freezes over in October, and remains so until July.

A COLD AND BEAUTIFUL LAND

In the High Arctic islands, living communities of plants and animals are so sparse that most of the area is referred to as "polar desert." Even in summer, much of it appears to be a wasteland of broken rock and gravel, too cold, dry, and windy to support any life. A closer look modifies, even if it does not entirely dispel, this impression. Plants of a very restricted variety grow: mostly lichens, mosses, and some low herbs. In protected locations, snowdrifts may not melt from one year to the next.

Plant cover becomes more continuous the farther south one goes, through the more southerly islands like Baffin and Victoria and on to the mainland tundra. In summer, much of the Central Arctic looks like a slightly more austere version of the mid-continental prairies, with rich grassy meadows and low rolling hills. But everywhere species diversity is low. In all of the Arctic islands botanists have counted about 350 different plant species; in the Amazon basin the figure is almost a hundred times this number.

The long night of the Arctic winter is often brilliant with stars and moon, and spectacularly lit by the flickering northern lights.

Because they radiate heat, the ears of Arctic hares are smaller than those of their more southerly relatives, including the snowshoe hare of the northern temperate and subarctic zones, and the cottontail rabbit of the eastern United States.

ARCTIC SURVIVAL STRATEGIES

Low species diversity characterizes animal populations as well. Reptiles and amphibians (which cannot regulate their own body temperatures) are absent, while bird and mammal species are comparatively few. Some species, however, are represented by innumerable individual animals. Millions of seals and hundreds of thousands of walrus and whales spend at least part of the year in Arctic waters.

Of course any species adapted to the Arctic must make concessions to the cold, and to the scarcity of winter food. Some animals hibernate. Most others migrate. Each summer nearly a sixth of all the bird species of North America, Europe, and northern Asia travel to the Arctic, where tens of millions of birds breed and raise their young. But each autumn they return south. Hardly a dozen bird species are capable of wintering in the Arctic: ptarmigans, ravens,

a few birds of prey, all tough and well-plumed against the cold, capable of scrounging a living from the bitter snow.

Only a few mammal species remain awake and present during the Arctic winter. Most barrenground caribou migrate south, to winter in the northern forests. The Peary caribou of the High Arctic islands are too remote from these forests to make the journey, however. Instead they "tough out" the winter, pawing through the snow for a few lichens and mosses. To avoid freezing, they must dig deep into their reserves of fat, and by spring they are often skinny, enfeebled, and starved. Not surprisingly, they are much smaller than their more southerly cousins, lighter-coloured, and live in much smaller herds, for the land can barely support them.

Musk-ox are other year-round denizens. They too depend on stored fat, and of course on their immensely

Icebergs are produced where a glacier flows into the ocean. Eighteen thousand years ago, great ice sheets covered much of the Northern Hemisphere, including almost all of Canada. Today remnants persist in the islands of the Eastern Arctic, and especially on Greenland.

shaggy coats, which provide an almost perfect insulation from winter's icy blasts. Like the Peary caribou, their energy balance is crucial, and comparatively minor climatic changes can mean the difference between life and death.

IN THE ARCTIC SEAS

For marine mammals, ice coverage is one of the most serious winter problems. All sea mammals require air to breathe, and each has different abilities to deal with ice, particularly the extensive landfast ice characteristic of the narrow seas of the Central Arctic. Unlike the moving pack ice of more open oceans, landfast ice is solidly anchored to the shore and forms a flat, unmoving expanse up to two metres or more thick. In north Alaska or along the eastern coast of Baffin Island, landfast ice is usually restricted to shore margins and some well-protected bays. But in the Central Arctic, where there are fewer tides and currents, most winter ice is landfast.

And not many sea mammals can deal with it. Only the small ringed seal can thrive by keeping open a network of breathing holes through the ice. Bearded seals also use breathing holes occasionally, but other Arctic sea mammals are normally associated with open pack ice. Few stray into the remote waters of the Central Arctic, even in summer.

Aside from the problem of ice, the sea is a kindlier host than the land. Arctic sea mammals are all carnivorous, and food is often abundant. Most seals, walrus, and small whales feed on fish, clams, octopuses, oysters, and various crustacean macro-plankton. Bowhead whales, the largest of all, feed entirely on microscopic krill, sieving the oceans through the great sheets of baleen in their mouths.

The Arctic cold is also less of a problem than on land. Temperature differences are far less extreme, fluctuating only a few degrees on either side of 0° C (sea water begins to freeze at about -3° C). Sea mammals can afford to sacrifice the insulation value of a heavy coat. Instead, they are protected by a thick mantle of blubber, weighing up to one-third of their total weight. It is this blubber that makes sea mammals such attractive prey, for it is one of the richest of all foods. A polar bear in good shape will eat only the blubber of the seals it kills, leaving the far less valuable meat for the foxes. Human beings too crave the calories that blubber can supply, both for themselves and as fuel for their lamps.

The seas are richer than the land, and most human life in the Arctic has clustered along its coasts. The Inuit were content to leave more southerly regions to Kannakapfaluk's other children.

In the High Arctic islands nearest the North Pole, summer temperatures usually hover near the freezing point, and snow drifts often remain unmelted from one year to the next.

CHAPTER 2

IN HONOUR OF AKULUK

The sled slid easily over the sea ice. For hours, days — forever, it seemed — Akuluk, Kahina, and the dogs had been running, their lungs expanding and hearts beating in unison as though they were incapable of stopping, gliding through the immense blue space and the silence. The only sound was the soft hiss of the runners and the crunch of paws on the firm snow.

Although many marriages were fragile at the beginning, divorce was rare after the birth of the first child.

Kahina trotted in front of the dogs. They were good dogs, well fed and strong. Akuluk had had Agluak with him when he came to Noahognir for the first time — a big, well-muscled dog, with an almost black coat, named for Akuluk's grandfather . The other dog, Kaumaq, he had picked up at Akilinik. He was a young and playful animal that nipped at everything. Akuluk ran behind the dogs, with a firm hold on the harness.

Straight ahead, was a thin line on the horizon — the large island that was their destination. They might be there by tomorrow. From there, they would follow the low hills of its coastline for days and days until they reached Kanghiryuak. They would no doubt have to search on the sea ice for some time to find the village. A man who was gone so long was sure of only one thing: his world would no longer be where he had left it.

Akuluk was happy to be going home. Every morning, as he re-iced and burnished the runners of the sled, he began to hum. Sometimes he laughed out loud for no reason. And then Kahina thought of her own parents, whom she wouldn't see again until the following winter, or perhaps ever. She told herself that there was already no sign left of her at Noahognir, nothing but memories in the minds of her parents, her brother, and the friends who had come to see her the morning she had left.

They had sat around her on the platform at the back of the snowhouse, holding her hands and looking at her. Her mother was there at the centre of things, just as she had been since the days when she had chewed pieces of seal meat to put in Kahina's mouth. But now, Kahina wasn't hungry. No one was hungry.

Her dear friend Koptana, her more-than-sister, was the first to arrive. Koptana was round and merry, and a very popular lover. Usually she was cheeky, but that morning, she was as serious as everyone else.

Pretty Kaniak was there too. Poor Kaniak. She had married a good hunter, Itaqlik, but he was at least twice her age, and on top of that he had another woman who made life difficult for Kaniak.

Agara had the worst time of all. She arrived that morning with a black eye and a split lip. Her husband had beaten her again. He was a lazy scoundrel with a violent temper. And he was always after other women. This marriage wouldn't last — Agara knew it as well as anyone.

As the sled sped over the sea ice, Kahina wondered if Akuluk would beat her. Even men who seemed gentle sometimes beat their wives. Koptana swore that if Naneoroak ever tried to beat her, she'd leave him. That was easy to say when you

still had your father or brothers to run to. Kahina, on the other hand, would have to walk for days and days to get to hers.

But she wasn't too worried. She would never give Akuluk reason to beat her. She was a good seamstress. All the women in Noahognir said so. She could already make a tent cover, straps and thongs, and even, with a little help, a kayak cover. She would keep the lamp going so that by the time he came home from the hunt, the seal would be almost cooked. And she would love him as much as he liked. Her cousin Punniq had taught her about this.

Making a son, however, was something else again. A woman could never know what she was carrying in her belly. It could well be that she would give her husband only girls. And then, even if he was gentle and tender, he would have every reason to beat her, put her out, or take up with another woman.

The day they left Noahognir, Kahina's mother fastened some *atagtat* to her clothes. "Wear them for the son you will have," she told Kahina. And then she told them the terrible story of Nitiksiq. She was very beautiful, and her husband was the best hunter in Noahognir. He had been found dead last summer, during the caribou hunt, his head fractured like a tern egg. They had never seen Nitiksiq again, and they probably never would. "Be careful," Kahina's mother warned.

Kahina tried not to worry. Every night before going to sleep, she sifted through the happy memories of the big party her parents had given in honour of Akuluk. Everyone had been there, in the big dance house: the children, the old people, the dogs. Kahina had worn her best clothes and her hair had been parted in the middle, smoothed back, and gathered into a big bun by Koptana. After a feast, they had played games and danced for a

A Quebec Inuit family photographed in 1902, during a visit to a trading post in the Ungava District.

Ikpakhuak, a respected Copper Inuit hunter, and his wife, Higilak, adopted the anthropologist Diamond Jenness. They taught him as much as they could about their culture during the nearly two years he lived with them.

long time to the beat of the drums. Akuluk had given Kahina's mother exactly what she wanted: a big iron cooking pot. He presented it to her in front of everyone, so they would know that he was wealthy and generous.

The next day, everyone had come out to say goodbye and to admire the sled. It was narrow and very long, made of wood, more stable and solid than all the sleds in Noahognir. Akuluk had it piled high with treasures he had brought back from Akilinik: pieces of wood that were almost as long as the sled, iron pots, harpoon points, very sharp snow knives, a few large caribou antlers, caribou blankets, and two big rocks for making lamps, which he had packed at the very back of the sled. On top of that, there were provisions for the trip and his weapons ready to hand. In spite of the heavy load, the iced runners slid lightly, leaving shallow grooves that were barely visible on the wind-hardened snow.

When it was time to leave, he had seated Kahina on the sled and they had glided away, but once the village had shrunk into the distance, he had signalled for her to get down. She had expected this; the dogs had to use their strength for pulling the big load.

The days were still quite short, but as long as there was light in the sky, they kept moving. On the ice, there were almost no obstacles — just a few ridges here and there, occasional crevasses like long scars in the ice, some hillocks cast in sharp relief by the sun — and they could move freely for long periods. Sometimes Akuluk would grab onto the back of the sled, brace his feet against the runners, and encourage his dogs with his voice, while Kahina ran beside the team. Together they established a steady rhythm that moved them across the top of the world.

27

A Marriage of Necessity

Like other Inuit, the Copper Inuit did not value celibacy. Marriage was not an option, but a matter of life and death, the union of a hunter and a seamstress. Neither could live without the contribution of the other. To eat regularly, to be adequately clothed, to survive day by day, to raise children, to feel the approach of old age with some security — all this required a spouse.

This beautifully decorated comb was made by the Thule-culture ancestors of the Copper Inuit, and is about 800 years old. It is made of walrus ivory, probably imported from the Western Arctic.

A man with no one to cook for him or sew his clothes was a terrible burden to his relatives. Poorly dressed, he froze when hunting on the sea ice in winter. In spring and summer his feet blistered in poorly repaired, soaking-wet boots. He had no tent, no cover for his kayak, no case for his bow. If despite all these handicaps he still managed to kill a caribou or seal, he had to butcher it himself, while other men were sitting at home eating dinner. Forced to depend on the charity of others, a man without a woman was hardly a real man at all.

It was the same for a woman. Without a man, where would she get food or hides for clothing? Although the Inuit were (and are) among the most generous people on earth, they went hungry with some frequency, and those who could not look after themselves were inevitably the first to do without. Man or woman, one had to marry.

In this context it is easy to see why physical attraction or romance counted for little compared with the more practical virtues of skill, perseverance, and hard work. A man might marry someone considerably older if she were a skilled seamstress. And often a young woman would prefer an older, successful hunter to a younger man she could not count on.

The marriage itself was not sanctioned by any particular ceremony. The couple simply lived together openly and that was that. They might set up their own independent household. Or if they were young, they might live for awhile with his family or, more often, hers, perhaps in an addition built onto the side of the parental snowhouse. A young wife could always use her mother's advice. Should they decide to move away

from the area, it was considered good manners for the husband to give his parents-in-law a gift to compensate for the loss of their daughter. And it was good manners for them to throw a party to say good-bye.

Some marriages were arranged long in advance. Cousin marriages of this sort were particularly common in some areas. Two sisters or perhaps two friends might promise that their children would marry, sometimes even before the children were born. These kinds of marriages were known but not strongly supported among the more western Copper Inuit, but were more popular farther east, around Bathurst Inlet. Yet such betrothals were never absolutely binding. Ultimately, people were free to marry whomever they wished, unless of course it was a case of incest. No one could marry a sibling or parent.

A man could have as many wives as he wanted, or at least as many as he could keep. In practice it was very rare to have more than one, since even the best hunter would have trouble supporting two families. Jealousy was also a problem, both between the wives and between the man and his fellows, some of whom might not have a wife at all. A woman might also have two husbands. It was perfectly permissible; indeed, it was no one's business except the participants. But hostility

between the men usually kept such unions very unstable.

Marriage by abduction was not uncommon, although only in the case of women who had already been married. No one would dare to carry off an unmarried girl against her own wishes or those of her parents. But a man might carry off a widow (who was considered a burden on her relatives anyway), or he might even deprive another man of his wife, although such events could lead to murder. Bullying too was not unheard of. A young man without any particular standing in the community might easily lose a wife to someone older and more powerful. This would be a very humiliating experience, and one that might drive the young man to seek revenge.

There were naturally degrees of abduction. A woman might not be altogether averse to being carried off. Indeed, the abductor must count on winning her over eventually, since no man could hope to keep a woman indefinitely against her will, and there was no social pressure forcing a woman to remain in a marriage that did not suit her.

Predictably, marriage was at its most fragile during the early stages. The longer a marriage lasted, the longer it was likely to last, and very few marriages broke up after the birth of the first child. Older couples usually treated each other with great kindness and respect.

When it did occur, divorce was as simple as marriage. No ceremony was required to begin a relationship nor was one required to end it. Women were not the chattels or slaves of their husbands and either party could instigate a break-up for any reason or in any way that seemed suitable. The tools and implements that a woman used belonged to her personally: ulus, scrapers and other sewing equipment, the cooking pot and lamp, her own clothing, the drying rack and other household furniture, and possibly one or more of the dogs and the spring tent. The man would have his clothes, his hunting and manufacturing gear, the sled, and the kayak if there was one. Any children normally went with the mother.

Although divorce was not a social disgrace, it did cause added hardship. One or both parties would find themselves alone, without a spouse, and would be forced by circumstances to live with relatives, perhaps parents or a married sibling. Inevitably, they would try to remarry as quickly as possible, because a happy, respected person was a married person.

A woman sews while her husband sits beside her on the sleeping platform, putting the finishing touches on a soapstone cooking pot. During the winter, most of a woman's tasks took place indoors.

A Union of Skills

The work of society was apportioned between the sexes. For a married couple to live well, each partner had to understand and uphold his or her proper role. Each sex had its tasks, its domains of responsibility, and its specialized skills. It was the union of these skills and duties that made life comfortable and happy.

The sexual division of labour in traditional Inuit society followed rules that would be familiar to most people. Men performed tasks that depended on strength and agility, particularly those concerned with hunting. Women were assigned the domestic duties such as cooking, sewing, and looking after children. The realm of women was in the house, while that of men was outdoors. The two sexes thus complemented rather than duplicated each other; they were two halves joined to make a whole.

Most of a man's duties revolved around his role as hunter and chief provider for his family, a role that demanded a great deal of work and the ability to withstand hardship. In winter, weather permitting, the men went out seal hunting every day, often for eight or ten hours at a stretch, or longer if necessary. In bad weather men often had unhealed frost sores on their faces for weeks at a time, as the need for food forced them to brave even the coldest winds. There was no let-up in summer, when perpetual daylight meant they might be gone for twenty-four hours at a time. Hunting was a full-time job. Most other hunting societies in the world had some access to vegetable foods, invariably gathered by the women. In these societies, men normally had far more leisure time than women. This was not true among the Inuit.

Men also built the snowhouse and erected the heavy spring tent. They made most of the tools, both their own and those used by their wives: everything from kayak frames to sleds or copper-bladed scrapers. They also produced toys and dolls for their children, and sometimes helped around the house. Although it was supposedly beneath men's dignity to assist their wives with the autumn clothing, they nonetheless might often be found scraping hides if the need

was great. In the privacy of his own small summer camp, a man might even help gather fuel for cooking, a task that normally fell to small children.

But if providing the seal or caribou was the man's duty, once it was brought home the animal fell exclusively within the woman's domain. She butchered it and shared it out among their friends and neighbours according to more or less strict rules of precedence. By her generosity in this matter, she protected her husband's reputation, as well as her own. Women treated and sewed the hides, processed and cooked the meat, fueled and trimmed the lamps, and of course did most of the child rearing.

This division of labour was real but it was not foolishly strict. Not all women's work was domestic. They did much of the fishing, especially during the spring when jigging through the ice was the usual technique (spearing was normally reserved for the men). Communal caribou drives required their active participation. A few of the younger women, particularly those without children, sometimes even went caribou or seal hunting with the men. Women also had active, demanding roles while travelling or moving camp, helping to build the snow-

Drying rack support

house and pull the winter sled. When packing gear on their backs during the summer, the woman generally carried her own and her husband's sleeping gear, the lamp (if one was needed), and the cooking pot. Her husband carried the tent and his own tools and weapons. Either might pack a small, tired child, although a baby would be carried by its mother.

In an emergency, most men could duplicate their wives' more basic skills with thread and needle. In their turn, women were often remarkably good at what was normally considered men's work. Several traditional Inuit stories tell of women who for various reasons found themselves alone in winter without a husband or other male support. The narrator usually seems pleasantly surprised by their success in surviving. But specialization allowed a married couple together to command more skills than either one of them could individually.

Women probably came as close to full equality with men in traditional Inuit society as they ever have anywhere before very recent times. As we have seen, a woman owned property independently of her husband, and was ultimately a free individual able to make her own choices. She was mistress in her own house, where her authority was complete. Her husband was bound to discuss all important matters with her, such as proposed camp moves or plans on where to spend the summer. Her opinion was heard in the dance house when deliberations were in progress, and even on the hunting field when caribou were sighted and a drive was to be organized. After menopause, some women became shamans, and thus obtained considerable spiritual influence within the community. The position of women was probably highest during the summer, when people were living in small, intimate camps and behaviour was less formal, less governed by the rules of male pride than during the winter.

Nevertheless, as in all human societies, women were sometimes the victims of male violence. Many, perhaps most, men beat their wives at least occasionally, although judging by the reports of visitors it seems to have been a comparatively rare event. A black eye was quickly forgiven. If the damage was worse, at least the woman was under no social obligation to stay and be beaten again.

In winter the woman usually awoke first to light the lamp, while her husband and children lolled in the warmth of the family bed.

Caribou-skin blankets

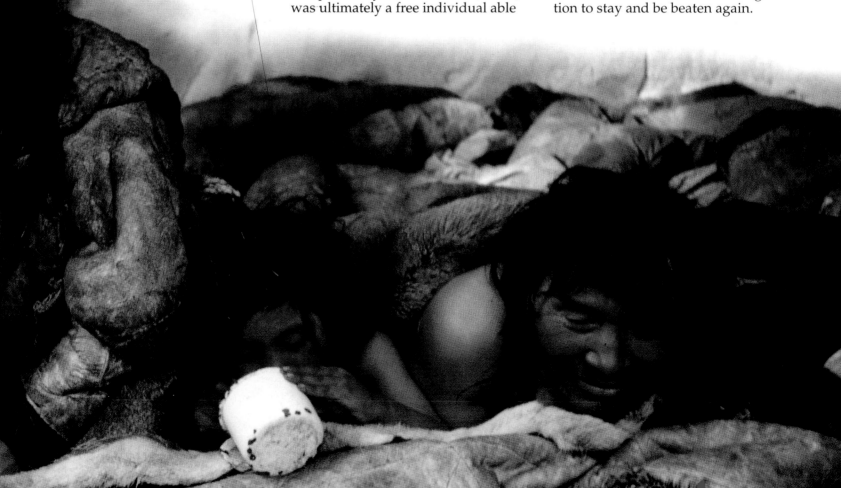

BEYOND THE TIES OF BLOOD

The nuclear family formed the basis of Inuit society nearly everywhere. This was particularly true among the Copper Inuit, where the first principle of social organization was a fierce egalitarianism unequaled elsewhere in the Arctic.

Nuclear families made up the individual building blocks from which larger communities were composed, but in these communities the family remained independent. No institutions or organizations transcended the family: no clans or lineages, no chiefs, no police, no government whatsoever beyond the free consent of individual households.

Copper Inuit society was at its most fragmented during the summer. Summer bands usually comprised two or three nuclear families, and sometimes only one, wandering across the interior tundra hunting and fishing. Families living together ordinarily consisted of close friends or relatives. Band composition fluctuated constantly, as individual families grouped and regrouped. The independence of the nuclear family was at its most obvious in this season.

People were also members of named regional groups, like Kahina's Noahognirmiut. These groups comprised all the people who normally summered in a particular area, and made up the pool from which the various smaller summer bands were drawn. Regional group names normally ended in the suffix *miut*, meaning "the people of" a particular place. The Noahognirmiut, for instance, were "the people of Noahognir," a place-name encompassing the area north of the Rae River, around the western end of Coronation Gulf. In Kahina's day (around 1910) there were about twenty of them, one of the smallest Copper Inuit bands. The Kanghiryuarmiut, Akuluk's people, were by far the largest, numbering almost two hundred.

Regional bands normally camped together for several weeks in autumn on the sea coast, to sew the winter clothing and await the freezing of the ocean. In spring they might get together again as the large winter villages dispersed for the summer. There were about seventeen such groups among the Copper Inuit at the beginning of this century. Although people were free within certain limits to move from one regional band to another, the core group within a band tended to be very similar from one year to the next.

The largest congregations usually occurred during the winter, when anywhere from ten to thirty families (perhaps 50 to 150 people) might live together in snowhouses on the sea ice. At this time of year people depended on breathing-hole seal hunting, which could support villages of this size, but only for a period of a month or so at any given location. As the local hunting fell off, villages would move en masse to a new location, usually somewhere relatively close by.

Most winters about eight such villages were dotted across the ice of

Large winter villages gave plenty of scope for an active social life, especially when different families joined their snowhouses together around a common dance house.

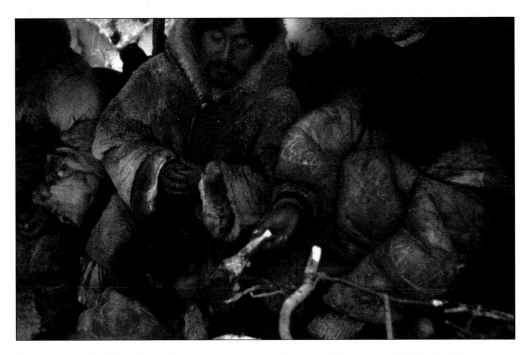

Inuit children were treated royally. They were allowed a great deal of freedom, and had few duties beyond learning (through games and imitation) what would be required of them as adults.

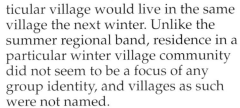

Coronation Gulf and up the western side of Victoria Island, nearly all consisting of the better part of several regional bands living together. Individual families, however, were free to make their own decisions about where to live, and only about two-thirds of the inhabitants of a particular village would live in the same village the next winter. Unlike the summer regional band, residence in a particular winter village community did not seem to be a focus of any group identity, and villages as such were not named.

The Copper Inuit lived with as little government as any people on earth. Yet it should not be assumed that they lived in a state of anarchy, without real community or society above the basic level of man and wife. A number of strong ties linked families in a wide network of friendship and mutual support. Kinship was not particularly important, although it did create strong relationships, especially between people who grew up in the same nuclear family.

Most social bonds, however, were with non-kin, or with people so distantly related that the kinship tie was irrelevant. The most important of these non-kinship ties were voluntary partnerships linking two individuals, usually men, and their families. There were three kinds of recognized partnerships: spouse-exchange partners, food-sharing partners, and dance partners. Together with simple, informal friendship, they provided the cement that held society together. Copper Inuit communities were real communities, not merely groups of people who happened to be living near one another.

A Perfect Expediency

Like Inuit social structures, the snowhouse was a temporary and multifaceted construction. Abandoned in spring, it slowly melted into nothingness, like the snowbanks around it or the sea ice upon which it stood. Like much of Inuit culture, it was an expediency — extremely functional, even beautiful, yet made almost from nothing. For many people the snowhouse is the perfect symbol of Inuit technology. Yet most Inuit never lived in one.

Copper Inuit snow shovel. A loop handle allowed it to be used with both hands.

In the Western Arctic, as in Greenland or Labrador, houses were normally made from more durable materials: sod and rock over a framework of driftwood or whale bone. Some dwellings had a separate kitchen for cooking over an open fire; some had a long entrance tunnel; some had no tunnel at all. They ranged in size from the small, single-family houses of north Alaska to the great communal houses of southwest Greenland. They too were igloos, for in the Inuit language the word *iglu* simply means a house of any sort.

Nearly everywhere, except in Alaska where it was unknown, the snowhouse was used mainly as a temporary dwelling, something that could be quickly thrown up when needed, on a long journey or when caught by a sudden blizzard. It is only in the Central Arctic, among the Copper Inuit and their neighbours that people lived the whole winter in snowhouses. And no wonder. For on the sea ice, what other building material is there besides snow?

The snowhouse was an almost perfect marriage of form and function. The basic shape is universally familiar: a dome made from blocks of snow, with a long tunnel for a door. The dome is based on the true

arch expanded into three dimensions, the only use of this architectural form in aboriginal North America. Its chief advantages are strength and the ability to hold up a roof without internal supports. Four or five adults can stand on the roof of a properly made snowhouse without any danger of damaging it.

As well as strength, a snowhouse was designed for warmth and comfort, particularly if it was intended as more than a temporary living space. A block of freshwater ice set in the roof provided light. The entrance tunnel would be very long, perhaps 10 or 15 metres, and built at right angles to the prevailing winds. It would also be the lowest part of the house, coming into the interior floor from below. Because cold air sinks and warm air rises, not even the breath of a draft would get through. In fact so effective was this "cold trap," that even if the tunnel was left unblocked it was usually necessary to cut a small ventilation hole in the roof.

Snow provides very good insulation, but only within certain obvious limits. It is not practical to heat a snowhouse much above the freezing point, or the walls begin to

Entrance tunnel

Inuit residing around the mouth of the Mackenzie River lived in large, comfortable multifamily houses framed with driftwood. The usual style, shown here, was occupied by three families, each having its own raised sleeping alcove, clustered in a clover-leaf fashion around a central living area.

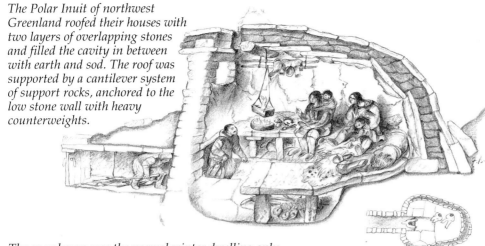

The Polar Inuit of northwest Greenland roofed their houses with two layers of overlapping stones and filled the cavity in between with earth and sod. The roof was supported by a cantilever system of support rocks, anchored to the low stone wall with heavy counterweights.

The snowhouse was the normal winter dwelling only in the Central Arctic, where the rarity of wood and a migratory lifestyle made the permanent sod, rock, and driftwood houses of other areas impractical.

drip. But cold is relative, and an inside temperature of +5° C can seem quite comfortable when it is 40 or 45 degrees colder outside.

Building with snow blocks encouraged architectural flexibility. Two or sometimes three snowhouses could be joined in a spirit of friendliness between families. Houses could share an entrance tunnel or be linked even more intimately by merging side walls, so that from the outside they looked like scoops of ice cream piled together.

Window made from a block of ice

Ventilation hole

Drying rack

Cooking pot

Lamp

Sleeping platform

BUILDING WITH SNOW

Snowhouse construction was made possible by the nature of Arctic snow. It is not that there is a lot of it; the Arctic is a very dry place, and only a few dozen centimetres fall every winter. Southern Canada has far more snow. What makes Arctic snow unique is its texture: hard, dense, and windpacked, easy to walk on, and, sometimes, perfect for building. In lands more blessed with trees and less blessed with wind the snow lies soft and powdery on the ground, nearly as treacherous to walk on as quicksand, and about as useful.

Bone or antler handle

Sealskin lashing

Raw copper blade

The style and material of this snowknife are peculiar to the Copper Inuit. Elsewhere in the Arctic, snowknives were usually curved, and made in one piece of bone or antler.

For two-thirds of the year, the Inuit lived in a world of ice and snow. They built their houses from it, sledded on it, hunted seals through it. It is not surprising that it occupied a large place in their thoughts. All languages have technical vocabularies, and the Inuit are justly famous for the many words describing the various states and forms of frozen water. For them it was a severely practical exercise; language reflects what a people must know. Here are some of the words for snow in Inuinnaqtun, as the Copper Inuit dialect of the Inuit language is called.

aniu: good snow to make drinking water
apiqqun: first snow in autumn
apun: fallen snow
aqilluqaq: fresh soft snow
mahak: melting snow
minguliq: falling powdered snow
natiruvik: snow blowing along a surface
patuqun: frosty sparkling snow
pukak: sugar snow
pukaraq: fine sugar snow
qaniaq: light soft snow
qanik: snow flake
qanniq: falling snow in general
qayuqhak: snowdrift shaped by the wind, resembling a duck's head
ukharyuk, qimugyuk, aputtaaq: snowbank

Building with snow was primarily a man's job. The principal tool was a *pana*, a snow knife about 35 centimetres long and, among the Copper Inuit, copper-bladed. Also useful were a shovel and a snow probe, a long stick of antler used for determining the consistency of a snow drift.

The first step was to find the right kind of snow, using the probe to check likely looking drifts.

The snow had to be hard and dense, uniform enough not to split, and deep enough for good, thick blocks. Often in early winter it was impossible to find good snow deep enough for building. Then people huddled together in their frigid tents and prayed for snow, or improvised with blocks of ice.

To provide light during the short winter day, the builder trims a window of freshwater ice to set over the door of the snowhouse.

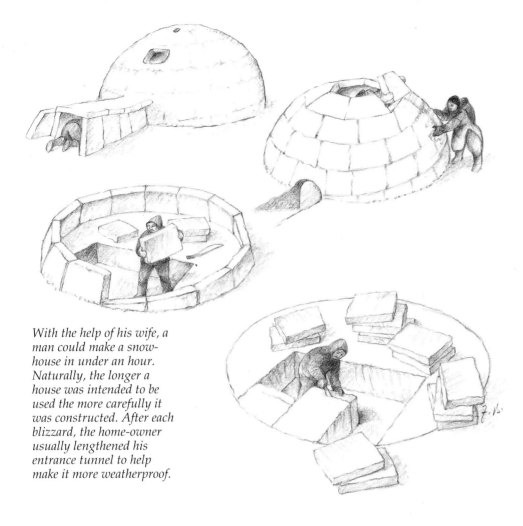

With the help of his wife, a man could make a snow-house in under an hour. Naturally, the longer a house was intended to be used the more carefully it was constructed. After each blizzard, the home-owner usually lengthened his entrance tunnel to help make it more weatherproof.

Copper Inuit snow shovel. Made of wood, it has a loop handle and an antler or bone edging. The cracked blade has been mended in several places with a sinew stitching.

Leather handle

Antler edging

Having found his drift, a man would begin to cut rectangular snow blocks with his knife. As much as possible, blocks were cut from the interior of the house, since the deeper the floor the lower the roof could be. Work proceeded from the inside.

The arrangement of the first tier of blocks naturally determined the size of the house. Beginning with the second tier, the blocks spiralled upward and inward. Blocks were arranged so that the joints between them came in steps, no block lying exactly over the one beneath. As the wall sloped in toward the apex the exact fit between blocks became more important, since each block had to support the one next to it. If a good dome were not formed the roof would be too flat and might fall in. The final block was the most critical, held in place with the left hand and trimmed to fit exactly. The door was then cut and the builder emerged, well pleased, it is hoped, with his creation.

The structure was now complete, but full of holes where the blocks were improperly joined. These had to be chinked from the outside by stuffing small chunks of hard snow into the larger gaps, then filling all the joints with a mortar of soft snow.

While the man was working, his wife and children would build a low rampart around the house about 15 centimetres from the wall, and fill the gap with soft snow to keep draughts from the floor. The woman then went into the house with a shovel and levelled out the floor in the front half of the house, piling the snow in the back half to make a sleeping platform. Meanwhile, the man dug out and built the entrance tunnel, with (among the Copper Inuit) straight stacked walls roofed over with flat slabs. Once the furniture was moved in, the house was ready.

Because a snowhouse is a dome, the height is naturally determined by the diameter. Building a large communal dance house meant constructing a platform of snow blocks so that the builders could reach the roof. This was dispensed with for private dwellings, so that practical maximum dimensions were a diameter of about four metres and a height of about two.

A new snowhouse is one of the most beautiful of all buildings. Being a true dome, the proportions are perfect; but yet more beautiful is the light. By night a snowhouse glows from within, lit a warm yellow by the lamp. By day the inside is even more luminous, the snow walls warmer and richer than marble or alabaster. A snowhouse is like a hollow jewel.

Both the beauty and comfort of this jewel, however, decreased with the passage of time. Slowly the inside walls would blacken from the soot of even the best-tended lamp. The floor in front of the sleeping platform would inevitably become foul with the blood and general mess of seal butchering. And the walls would gradually ice up with condensing water vapour and the daily changes in inside temperature. As the house became dirtier it also became colder, since ice lacks the insulation qualities of dense snow. But none of this was a real problem, for the snowhouse was always meant to be temporary. After a month or so it was time to move.

This Dorset culture harpoon head is made of antler, and decorated with a carved human face. The stone end-blade is missing.

The Peoples of the Arctic
1. *Copper Inuit*
2. *Netsilik*
3. *Caribou Inuit*
4. *Sadlermiut*
5. *Iglulingmiut*
6. *Quebec Inuit*
7. *Labrador Inuit*
8. *Baffin Islanders*
9. *West Greenlanders*
10. *Polar Inuit*
11. *East Greenlanders*
12. *Saami*
13. *Nenets*
14. *Dolgan*
15. *Nganasan*
16. *Evenki*
17. *Yakut*
18. *Chukchi*
19. *Koryak*
20. *North Alaskan Inuit*
21. *Aleut*
22. *South Alaskan Yuit*
23. *Mackenzie Inuit*

THE TOP OF THE WORLD

The North American Arctic was the last major environment on earth to be occupied by human beings. It was only a little over 4,000 years ago that the first people entered this forbidding region.

Archaeologists call the earliest Arctic Americans "Palaeoeskimos," from *palaeo*, a prefix meaning "ancient." Their cultural remains have been found scattered from Alaska to Greenland: tiny, delicate stone tools of distinctive, particular forms, sometimes found in or around the ruins of a flimsy sod house or ring of stones that once held down the apron of a skin tent. Occasionally, in areas where preservation is unusually good, some of the more perishable products of this long-vanished culture are also in evidence: discarded animal bones, and tools made of antler, ivory, or wood.

We can only guess why the Palaeoeskimos began their epic trek into the frigid and treeless islands of the High Arctic and Greenland, and into the continental tundra west of Hudson Bay. They must have been a hungry people, used to cold and hardship and a way of life that demanded constant movement from one place to another just to wring a living from a sparse land.

THE DORSET

The early Palaeoeskimo period in the Eastern and Central Arctic lasted for over a thousand years, a period when the form of various tools slowly changed as different styles came and went. But during the centuries between about 3,000 and 2,500 years ago, the pace of change seems to have quickened. New tool types appeared, including the first stone lamps. Substantial winter houses were developed, often dug into the ground to help conserve heat. The places where people lived changed too, as they clustered more and more on the coast, abandoning the continental interior to incoming Indians. Even the bow and arrow seems to have been lost or forgotten. The culture that emerged from all these changes is known to archaeologists as "Dorset," named for Cape Dorset on southern Baffin Island, where it was first recognized. The distribution of Dorset culture has been traced from east Greenland as far west as the country of the Copper Inuit, and into the High Arctic islands to the limits of human habitation.

In comparison with the culture of the earliest Palaeoeskimos, Dorset culture seems more familiar, more like that of recent Central Arctic Inuit. Dorset people may have invented the snowhouse, for instance, and they seem to have perfected the art of hunting seals at their breathing holes through the winter ice. Blubber lamps and better housing suggest a more comfortable, less precarious existence. Their kitchen middens are thick and rich, full of animal bones, and their village sites larger and more crowded than those of their predecessors.

Dorset culture is recent enough that in many areas of the Arctic tools made of wood, ivory, and antler survive to the present day. Thus while we know almost nothing about early Palaeoeskimo art, we know a great deal about the art of Dorset people, mainly in the form of small wooden and ivory carvings. Dorset art is one of the most gripping and dramatic of all the so-called primitive arts in the world. Much of it seems to have been deeply preoccupied with the forces of magic and shamanism, reflecting the psychological insights upon which the Dorset probably depended for their spiritual survival.

THE SECOND WAVE: ALASKA AND THE THULE INUIT

While Dorset culture was unfolding in Canada and Greenland, late Palaeoeskimo people in Alaska were developing along their own paths. A

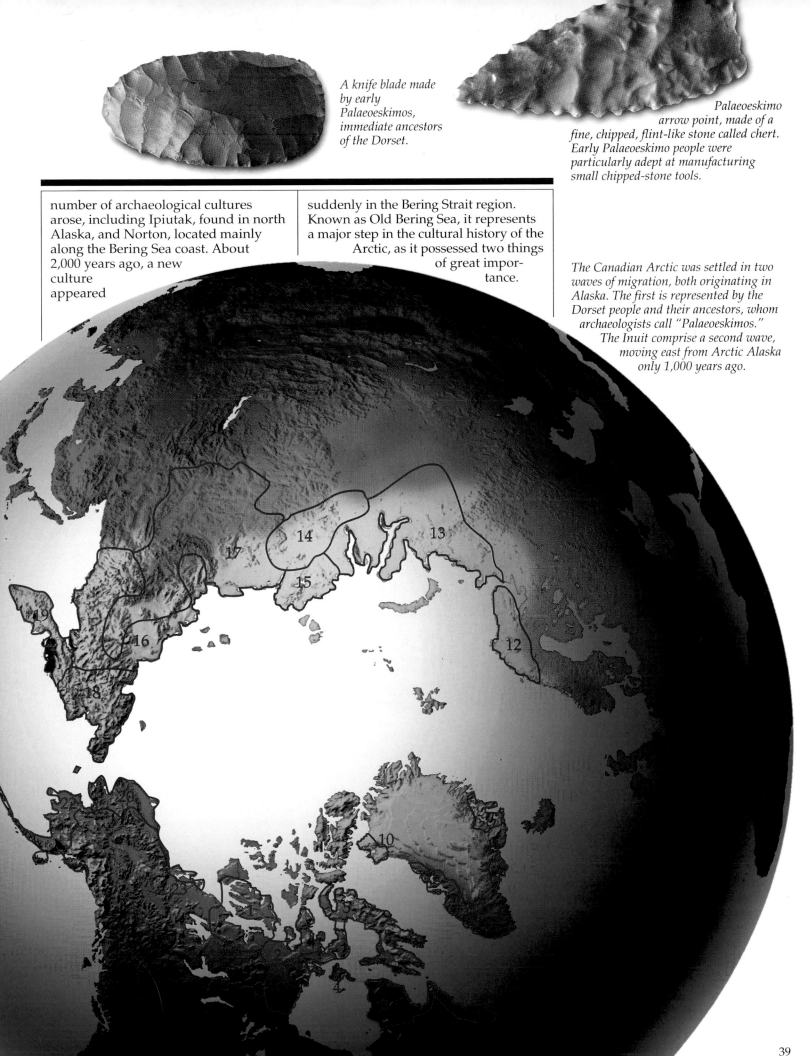

A knife blade made by early Palaeoeskimos, immediate ancestors of the Dorset.

Palaeoeskimo arrow point, made of a fine, chipped, flint-like stone called chert. Early Palaeoeskimo people were particularly adept at manufacturing small chipped-stone tools.

number of archaeological cultures arose, including Ipiutak, found in north Alaska, and Norton, located mainly along the Bering Sea coast. About 2,000 years ago, a new culture appeared suddenly in the Bering Strait region. Known as Old Bering Sea, it represents a major step in the cultural history of the Arctic, as it possessed two things of great impor-tance.

The Canadian Arctic was settled in two waves of migration, both originating in Alaska. The first is represented by the Dorset people and their ancestors, whom archaeologists call "Palaeoeskimos." The Inuit comprise a second wave, moving east from Arctic Alaska only 1,000 years ago.

Antler head

Raw copper blade

This harpoon head from the Copper Inuit region dates from a more settled phase of Thule culture, about 700 or 800 years ago. The use of copper has deep roots in the area.

Stone side-blade   *Walrus ivory*

Birnirk-culture harpoon head from northwestern Alaska, made of ivory with inset stone blades. Dating to about 1,400 years ago, Birnirk represents an early stage in the development of Inuit culture.

The style of this antler harpoon head indicates that it was made and used by the earliest Thule people to enter the Canadian Arctic, about 1,000 years ago.

Raw copper lance and arrow heads, Thule culture

One of these was smelted iron, first traded across Bering Strait from Siberia and China at this time. Old Bering Sea artists took advantage of iron-tipped tools to produce a major new art style, carved in walrus ivory. Cool, abstract and sophisticated, it seems to reflect a much more self-assured worldview than the stark primitivism of Dorset art.

Of greater importance was the invention of the inflated skin float. Attached to the harpoon head and thrown overboard when an animal was struck, it allowed for the first time the effective hunting of sea mammals in open water. With it, Old Bering Sea people and their descendants became perhaps the best sea mammal hunters in the world. Early experimentations led to greater and greater prowess, until eventually even the great baleen whales could be successfully hunted.

Old Bering Sea seems to represent the first clear step in a line of development leading to the culture of the modern Inuit. By the time of the succeeding Birnirk culture, we are almost certainly dealing with a people who spoke an early form of the Inuit language. For this is where the direct ancestry of the Inuit lies, not with Canadian Palaeoeskimo or Dorset. It was the next stage of Inuit cultural development, known to archaeologists as Thule (pronounced "Tooley"), that saw the spread of Inuit people and language throughout the Arctic. Beginning about a thousand years ago, the Thule Inuit began the most dramatic series of migrations in Arctic history. These migrations completely changed the ethnic map of the Arctic, bringing Inuit people east out of Alaska into Canada and Greenland at the expense of their distant relatives, the Dorset.

Reasons for this major population movement are, as it always seems, poorly understood. Social problems at home, such as overpopulation or endemic feuding, may have contributed. So too might a warming climate, which favoured the spread of both bowhead whales and bowhead whale hunters. By the end of the thirteenth century most of Arctic Canada and Greenland was in the hands of Thule Inuit.

They were not moving into unoccupied territory. In southwestern Greenland they met a far-flung and neglected extension of medieval Europe: the Norse colony founded by Erik the Red. By the time other European explorers arrived on the scene four or five hundred years later, the Norse were gone and only the Inuit inhabited Greenland.

Elsewhere in the Eastern Arctic they must also have met their distant relatives, the Dorset. The final outcome was the same; like the Norse, the Dorset disappeared. At key archaeological sites, places with a long history of Dorset occupation, the same pattern is repeated again and again. The Dorset occupation suddenly comes to an end, without any apparent reason. Very shortly thereafter (it is impossible to be more precise), Thule Inuit move onto the site, which they and their descendants continue to occupy until the present day.

It is difficult to know what complex reality is obscured by this simple pattern. Inuit oral histories tell of a people called the Tunit who occupied the Canadian Arctic when their ancestors first arrived. After a dispute, the Tunit fled and were never seen again.

A CULTURAL CRISIS

Thule culture of eight hundred or a thousand years ago represents a high point in Inuit history — a kind of Arctic golden age. Superb hunters, the Thule Inuit had the technology and skills to

Slate blade

Whale bone harpoon head

thrive almost everywhere in the Arctic. In many areas their summer whale hunting yielded enough food to support people throughout the winter in comparative ease, living in large, warm sod houses. Some of their villages contained fifty or sixty houses.

Yet this is not what nineteenth- and early twentieth-century European explorers found in the Central Arctic. Instead, they found snowhouse Inuit, people like Kahina and her relatives. The whole focus on whaling had disappeared, and with it the elaborate culture it supported, including a large seasonal food surplus and snug, permanent winter houses. What had happened?

A change in climate was probably partially to blame. Throughout much of the northern hemisphere, this period witnessed a marked decrease in temperature known as the Little Ice Age. Winters were colder than they are now, and much colder than they had been during the period of Thule expansion. Sleet on the spring calving grounds may have reduced caribou populations, while severe ice conditions in the narrow seas of the Central Arctic — always a relatively poor place — could have caused drastic reductions in the distribution and overall number of sea mammals. In more favoured regions like Alaska or southwestern Greenland, other Inuit were sometimes able to cope with the worsening climate of the Little Ice Age with greater ease. In the Central Arctic, however, increasing poverty and starvation may have resulted in the

much simpler cultures seen by European explorers.

Another factor that influenced the development of traditional Central Inuit culture was contact with Europeans. After the Norse, Western European sailors were visiting the Eastern Arctic at least as early as the sixteenth century. They probably brought with them European infectious diseases such as smallpox, influenza, and measles. Like other New World populations, the Inuit had no inherited resistance to these plagues, which we know were capable of reducing what are called "virgin soil" populations by as much as 90 or 95 percent. Documentary evidence from the Canadian Arctic earlier than about 1820 is exceedingly scarce, but it seems likely that many Inuit populations had already been badly hit by European diseases with presumably disastrous cultural consequences.

Inuit culture as seen by nineteenth- and early twentieth-century explorers was far from the "pristine" hunting culture often depicted. All human beings, even those who inhabit the most northerly regions, live in a world subject to change, and to history.

Two or three times the size of the other illustrated harpoon heads, this Thule culture specimen is about 500 or 600 years old, and was employed in hunting the enormous bowhead whales of the Arctic.

Walrus ivory

This Old Bering Sea harpoon head from Bering Strait, Alaska, is about 2,000 years old, and elaborately decorated. Old Bering Sea is the earliest archaeological culture that can be directly linked with the culture of recent Canadian Inuit.

Most Thule Inuit framed their winter houses with whale bone.

BAFFIN ISLAND

The Inuit of southern and eastern Baffin Island lived a more secure, prosperous life than did their countrymen farther west. Sophisticated sea mammal hunters living in a relatively rich environment, they pursued whales, walrus, and a variety of seal species. They lived in both permanent sod and wood houses, and in snowhouses when necessary. Baffin Inuit have had a long history of contact with Europeans, beginning (almost certainly) with the Norse. When Martin Frobisher sailed to their country in the 1570s he found them already well versed in the mechanics of European trade.

COPPER INUIT

The Copper Inuit exemplify the harsh living conditions of the Central Canadian Arctic. With their neighbours to the east, the Netsilik, they are the classic snowhouse Inuit of popular imagination, but are far from representative of Inuit culture in general. During the long local winters, they lived almost entirely by hunting ringed seals at their breathing holes through the sea ice. Spring and summer were spent on the land, hunting caribou and fishing. Unlike most other Inuit, they engaged in no open-water sea mammal hunting. With a homeland far from the major sea lanes and world centres of commerce, the Copper Inuit were among the last aboriginal people on earth to be absorbed into the global economy.

QUEBEC INUIT

The Inuit living to the south of Hudson Strait had a culture very similar to that of their neighbours to the north. One difference, however, was a greater reliance (by some) on terrestrial resources, chiefly fish and caribou, which they hunted in large drives. Before the 1930s, many hundreds of Quebec Inuit lived more or less permanently in the interior. Like other interior Inuit living in northern Alaska (the so-called Nunamiut) and in the Central Arctic (Caribou Inuit), they provide a contrast to a more maritime adaptation seen elsewhere in the Inuit world. Other Quebec Inuit were primarily sea mammal hunters, especially the inhabitants of the Belchers and other islands off the East Main, where polar bears, seals, and walrus were important food sources.

Copper Inuit

Baffin Island

Quebec Inuit

Saami

Yakut

West Greenlanders

SAAMI

The Saami (or Lapps as they were once called) live in far northern Europe, including Arctic Norway, Sweden, Finland, and the Kola Peninsula of far northwestern Russia. As early as A.D. 800 they were already keeping small herds of domesticated reindeer, and by late medieval times had become specialized reindeer herders, living off the meat and milk of their herds, and using them to pull sleds. Perhaps the first Eurasian Arctic people to make the crucial switch from hunting to herding, they share a number of important cultural traits with other circumpolar people, including traditional religious beliefs based on shamanism. Less than 10 percent of Saami now follow a traditional life-style.

WEST GREENLANDERS

Almost as specialized in sea mammal hunting as the Aleuts, the Inuit of West Greenland were colonized by the Danes in the 18th century. At first they were taken to be, at least in part, the descendants of the old Norse settlement in Greenland founded a thousand years ago by Erik the Red, the fate of which was unknown in Europe at the time. Instead, archaeological and archival research suggests that the ancestors of the Greenlanders were Thule-culture Inuit, who entered Greenland from the north about 800 years ago. Several centuries of benevolent Danish rule have protected the Greenlanders from the worst excesses of exploitation suffered by many other Arctic peoples.

YAKUT

The Yakut are the largest Native ethnic group in Siberia. They are a Turkic-speaking people, with both a language and house style betraying an origin in the steppe country of Central Asia, far to the south of their modern home in the Lena River drainage of north central Siberia. As well as reindeer, more southern groups keep both cattle and horses, domesticated animals they brought with them from Central Asia. They are also noted for their advanced iron-working techniques.

EVEN

Like most Siberian groups, the Even were (and continue to be) reindeer herders and hunters. Until very recent times, however, they were less dependent upon herding than many of their neighbours, with smaller herds valued chiefly for transportation rather than for meat and milk. As well as pulling sleds, reindeer were saddled and ridden like horses, a practice with origins in the steppe country to the south. The Even language belongs to the Northern (Tungus) subgroup of the Tunguso-Manchurian language family; related languages are spoken as far away as northern China.

NENETS

The Nenets of northwestern Siberia were (and are) long-distance migratory reindeer herdsmen, following their animals from their summer pastures on the Arctic tundra to wintering grounds within the boreal forest zone. Like the Saami, they are among the more highly specialized of Old World reindeer herders. Some groups summer as far north as the Arctic coast and engage in some sea mammal hunting. Fishing is also an important activity. Largely ignored by the Soviet and Russian governments, the Nenets still retain a great deal of their traditional culture, and follow a way of life little changed for centuries. They speak a Uralic language, distantly related to Saami, as well as to Finnish, Hungarian, and Estonian.

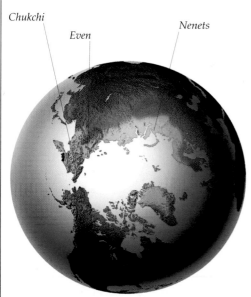

Chukchi

Even

Nenets

CHUKCHI

The Chukchi of far northeastern Siberia are divided into two groups: the Maritime Chukchi, who were sea hunters, and the Reindeer Chukchi, who were primarily reindeer breeders. They lived in a symbiotic relationship, exchanging sea mammal products (blubber, seal and walrus skins) for reindeer skins. The culture of the Maritime Chukchi, in particular, shares a number of traits with that of Alaskan Inuit, and some scholars have seen linguistic connections as well. More securely, the Chukchi language is grouped with Koryak in the Chukotko-Kamchatkan language family. Tough warriors, the Chukchi were a major bar to Tsarist Russian expansion into northeastern Siberia in the 18th century.

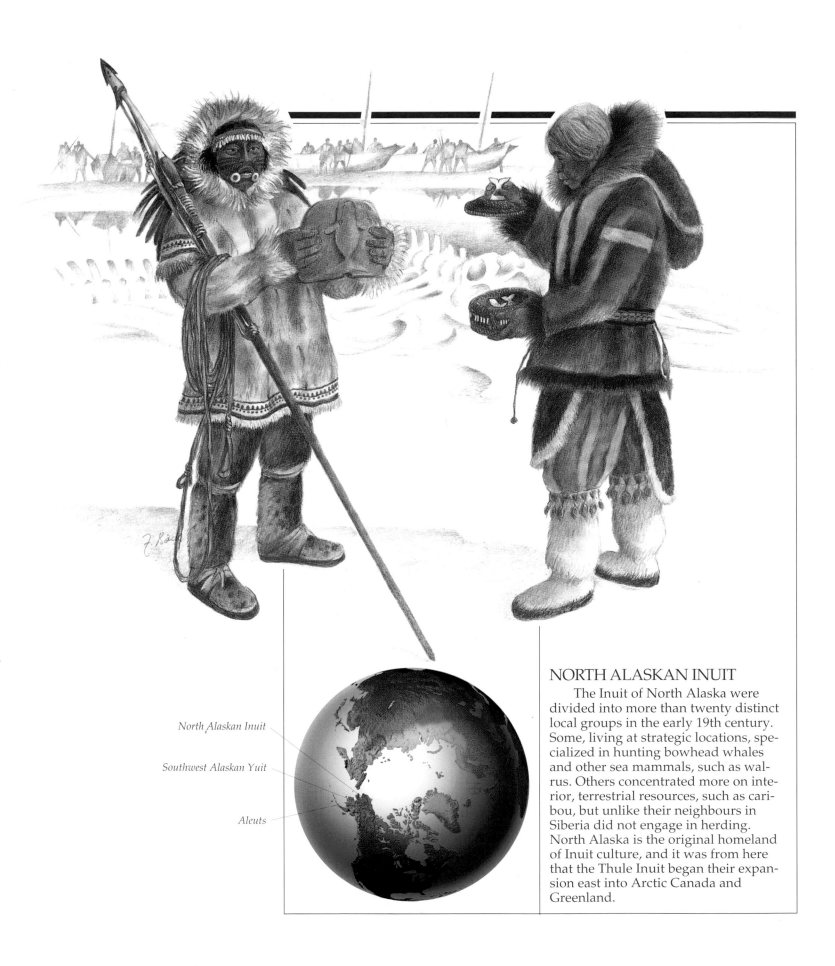

North Alaskan Inuit

Southwest Alaskan Yuit

Aleuts

NORTH ALASKAN INUIT

The Inuit of North Alaska were divided into more than twenty distinct local groups in the early 19th century. Some, living at strategic locations, specialized in hunting bowhead whales and other sea mammals, such as walrus. Others concentrated more on interior, terrestrial resources, such as caribou, but unlike their neighbours in Siberia did not engage in herding. North Alaska is the original homeland of Inuit culture, and it was from here that the Thule Inuit began their expansion east into Arctic Canada and Greenland.

ALEUTS

Distant linguistic relatives of the Inuit and Yuit, the Aleuts live on the Aleutian Islands along the North Pacific rim. They were highly specialized sea mammal hunters, living in a chilly, maritime, but not truly Arctic environment. Against the larger sea mammals like whales they used poisoned darts for hunting, and were perhaps the best kayakers in the world. Aleuts also led an elaborate ritual and social life. Their society was more hierarchical than that of most North American hunter-gatherers, and like their Amerindian neighbours of the Northwest Coast they kept slaves. Their culture was much changed by Russian colonization and exploitation in the 18th century.

SOUTHWEST ALASKAN YUIT

The "Eskimo" language family includes two main branches: Inuktitut, spoken by the Inuit, and Yupik, spoken by the Yuit, as the Native inhabitants of coastal Alaska south of Bering Strait are called. Like the Inuit, they lived in sod and driftwood winter houses, and hunted a variety of animals, particularly sea mammals. South of Bering Strait ice conditions are much less severe than farther north, so that most Yuit were able to specialize in open-water hunting nearly year-round. Population densities were high, especially south of the Alaskan Peninsula.

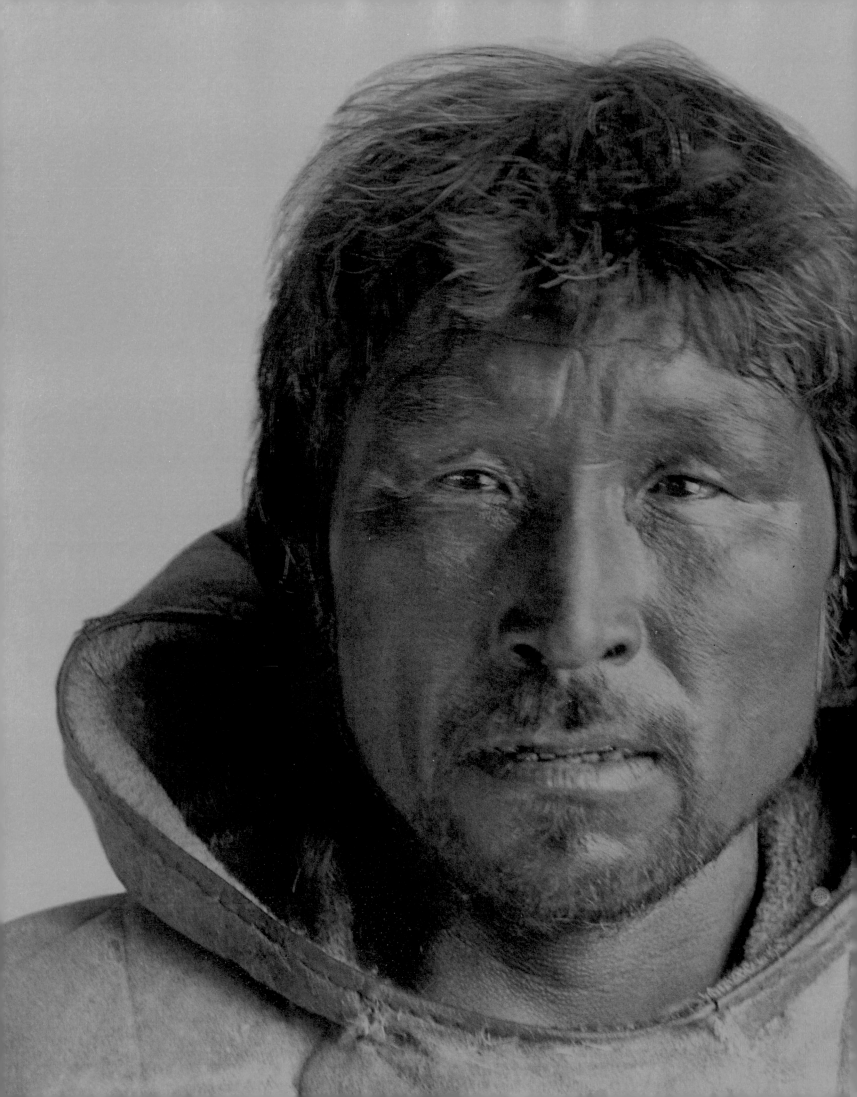

CHAPTER 3

VOICES OF THE DEAD

This wasn't the first time that Kahina had ever been hungry. Almost every year, during the coldest, darkest part of winter when blizzards blew for days on end, people knew the fear of famine.

Many Inuit men were tremendous travellers and had immense geographic knowledge, often spanning thousands of square kilometres. Travelling and hunting were constant, daily duties.

Everyone in Noahognir remembered one terrible winter that had been very cold and windy. Someone must have transgressed a taboo and refused to admit his or her fault, because in spite of the shaman's invocations and his trip to the bottom of the sea in an attempt to appease the spirits, the men had been unable to kill a single seal. Nothing, for days and days. They had had to eat skins — first the fresh ones, then the old, dried ones. Then they had eaten the lamp oil. Then they had killed and eaten the oldest dogs. An old woman died, then a child.... The warm days were late in coming, and even when the weather improved times were still hard, because the hunters had been weakened by the fast and no longer had dogs to help them find game. Worst of all, they were frightened.

But that had been a long time ago. In fact, Kahina wasn't certain if she really remembered this famine or just the stories she'd been told. It was still a major topic of conversation in Noahognir. Sometimes the elders whispered that they had known people who had eaten their dead. And it was said that in certain communities they had killed their children to feed themselves, though others said that it was to end their suffering.

Kahina knew hunger, but she wasn't used to fasting for any length of time. Nor was Akuluk, who had been sleep-

When Diamond Jenness lived among the Copper Inuit early in this century, they had the happy confidence of a people able to fulfil their own wants and needs.

ing almost all the time for two days and two nights in the little snowhouse he had built on the sea ice.

She dozed restlessly. It wasn't the hunger that she found hard to bear, but the inaction, the waiting, the uncertainty. She listened to the thick blizzard, its howling and muttering full of the voices of the dead — she clearly recognized the voices of her older brother, of a cousin who had also died on the hunt, of her grandmother. The other voices were those of many other dead people she hadn't known.

From time to time, Akuluk opened his eyes and listened, then pulled the blanket up over his shoulders and went back to sleep. He wasn't worried. Twice, he had prodded Kahina to relight the lamp. There was no need to skimp; they had enough oil to provide heat and light for days, and when one was forced to fast, it was better not to be too cold. So the little lamp burned almost continuously. But food was something else. At Puivlik, they had been given just enough to get to Hanerak, two days' walk away. As long as the blizzard was blowing and they couldn't travel, they had to fast.

Once, Kahina had tried to go out to take a look, but Akuluk had woken up and been very angry. He shoved her against the back of the snowhouse without saying a word. But she understood and was crestfallen and ashamed. Even a three-year-old knew that you could get lost in a blizzard just five or six steps away from the snowhouse. You could see nothing and hear nothing. Time stretched interminably!

They should have stayed at Puivlik, Kahina thought. The people hadn't been very kind or friendly, perhaps, but at least they would have been safe and sheltered there. It had been crazy to leave, when everyone could see that the blizzard was almost upon them. The sky had been a flat white, and the winds had swirled across the sea ice. But Akuluk had said that he was impatient to get home to Kanghiryuak; they weren't halfway there yet. He planned to rest at Hanerak before the hardest part of the journey, the five or six days' travel along the shore of the large island.

Kahina and everyone else knew the real reason: Akuluk didn't want to lend or exchange his young wife, not to the people of Puivlik, among whom he didn't feel comfortable. At Hanerak, he would be almost home, among his own, for he had cousins and friends there.

They had just left Puivlik when the blizzard began blowing in earnest. Akuluk had built this snowhouse, working almost by feel because he couldn't see anything. He had pushed Kahina inside, followed her, and lain down. For two days and two nights, they waited, sleeping a lot, making love, eating nothing, sometimes sliding into strange dreams.

Kahina dreamt that she and Akuluk were walking on the sea ice, their backs warmed by the sun. The sled was sliding along noiselessly, the dogs trotting. Suddenly, they saw footprints — their own footprints — ahead of them. When Kahina looked behind her, there was nothing. As soon as they placed their feet in the prints in the snow, all trace of where they had been disappeared. Kahina, stunned, turned toward Akuluk, who gave her a broad smile.

And then she woke with a start, struck by the silence. Akuluk was sitting up, listening. The blizzard had ended. They slipped into their clothes and went outside. Everything was calm and mild, just as it had been in Kahina's dream. The dogs were still curled up under the snow, where they had been sleeping the entire time. Very high in the sky was the family of stars that the Inuit call the Caribou. A little closer was the constellation called the Bear, followed by the Hunter's Dogs. The story of the world was spread out in the sky for anyone to read, Kahina thought.

Akuluk fed the dogs — not too much, for well-fed dogs run badly, especially after several days of fasting. The sun would rise soon. The days were already almost as long as the nights. With a little luck, they would be at Hanerak before the following night.

Sex and Friendship

Of the three kinds of partnerships linking families and individuals, spouse-exchange partnerships were probably the most important, and certainly the most famous. Under the guise of "wife lending," the practice was well publicized by early explorers and both shocked and greatly fascinated readers in Europe and North America. Condemned by moralists, it was held up as clear proof of Inuit depravity, and of their urgent need for the ministrations of Christian missionaries.

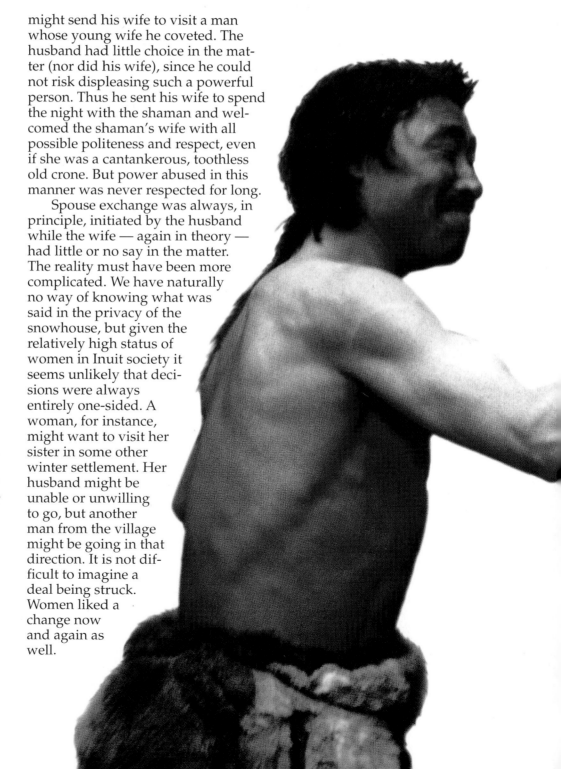

This Thule-culture "darting" harpoon head is made of antler. It is about 800 years old, and was almost certainly used for hunting small seals from a kayak.

On the other hand, the hospitable loaning of wives was also the object of voyeuristic envy and coarse bragging on the part of male, white Arctic explorers. These reactions, of course, tell us more about Western civilization than they do about the Inuit. Still, it is easy to understand why the topic remains a very sensitive one.

Spouse exchange was practised by most or all Inuit, including the Copper Inuit. As the moralists feared, it did sometimes serve no immediate function beyond the satisfaction of simple lust. Yet it also played a much greater role as one of the chief bonds that held society together.

To prevent conflict or to create friendly relationships, men would often exchange spouses on a temporary basis. A number of motives — some practical, some social, some frankly sexual — figured in the practice. A stranger entering a village would try to exchange wives with someone as quickly as possible in order to acquire a local sponsor. A hunter whose wife was ill or advanced in pregnancy might leave her in the care of a friend, and borrow the friend's wife for a long journey. Or close friends might simply desire a little sexual variety. Exchanges could take place for one night or for many nights, and might of course be repeated.

Spouse exchange should not be confused with adultery, however. What was offered in friendship should never be taken in treachery, and a woman who slept with another man behind her husband's back was asking for trouble.

Sometimes the practice was abused. A shaman, for example, might send his wife to visit a man whose young wife he coveted. The husband had little choice in the matter (nor did his wife), since he could not risk displeasing such a powerful person. Thus he sent his wife to spend the night with the shaman and welcomed the shaman's wife with all possible politeness and respect, even if she was a cantankerous, toothless old crone. But power abused in this manner was never respected for long.

Spouse exchange was always, in principle, initiated by the husband while the wife — again in theory — had little or no say in the matter. The reality must have been more complicated. We have naturally no way of knowing what was said in the privacy of the snowhouse, but given the relatively high status of women in Inuit society it seems unlikely that decisions were always entirely one-sided. A woman, for instance, might want to visit her sister in some other winter settlement. Her husband might be unable or unwilling to go, but another man from the village might be going in that direction. It is not difficult to imagine a deal being struck. Women liked a change now and again as well.

54

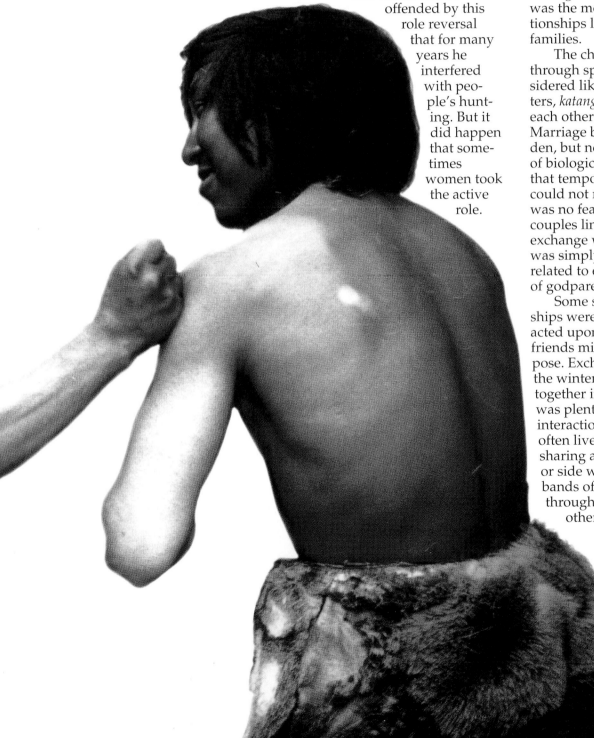

These Netsilik men are engaged in a punching duel, taking turns striking each other on the shoulder without attempting to defend themselves. The first one to give up loses. Formal duels like this were not practised by the Copper Inuit, although they did have a wide currency within the Inuit world. Smiles suggest that these men are just clowning around.

Normally, the women stayed in their own houses or tents, and the men did the visiting. There is a story told about two couples who wanted to exchange spouses, but for a little variety decided that this time the women would do the visiting. As they were going into each other's houses, the women were seen by a whale who was swimming close by the shore. The whale was so offended by this role reversal that for many years he interfered with people's hunting. But it did happen that sometimes women took the active role.

Perhaps more important than the immediate motive or manner of exchange was the outcome. Families who exchanged spouses established a partnership that could endure for life, no matter how brief the actual union. They could depend on each other for help in a crisis, for hospitality while travelling, and for general cooperation in daily living. Particularly among the Copper Inuit, this bond was the most important of all relationships linking different nuclear families.

The children of couples joined through spouse exchange were considered like adopted brothers and sisters, *katangotit*. They too could call on each other for help, even as adults. Marriage between them was forbidden, but not because it was a question of biological incest. The Inuit believed that temporary spouse exchanges could not result in pregnancy. There was no fear, then, that the children of couples linked through spouse exchange were actually siblings; it was simply that they were already related to each other, like the children of godparents in Catholic Europe.

Some spouse-exchange partnerships were of course more frequently acted upon than others, and close friends might often visit for the purpose. Exchange was most common in the winter, when people lived together in large villages and there was plenty of opportunity for social interaction. Closely linked couples often lived in adjacent snowhouses sharing a common entrance tunnel or side wall. The tiny, intimate bands of summer were often joined through spouse exchange as well as other ties.

Families linked through spouse exchange did not always live in the same settlement or band. In fact, there was a real practical advantage in having partners living in other regions, particularly if one were travelling or forced to move for some reason. There was no limit to the number of exchange partners a family could have.

SOCIAL PLACES

A new snowhouse was an especially beautiful dwelling, with its white, semitranslucent walls and flickering lamplight. The inside was divided in half by a raised sleeping platform along the back wall, made of piled snow and edged with blocks standing perhaps half a metre above the floor.

Blubber was beaten with this musk-ox horn blubber pounder, breaking the fat cells and releasing oil for burning in a lamp.

Musk-ox horn

Finger notches

The platform was usually provided with a mat of woven willow twigs covered by a mattress of heavy musk-ox robes and caribou-hide blankets or sleeping skins for bedding. People slept side by side, heads towards the entrance passage and feet against the rear wall. This arrangement made it easy for the housewife to lean over and light the lamp in the morning without getting out of bed.

Winter was a very social time. A large winter village offered tremendous scope for visiting and gossiping after the tiny camps of summer. During the day, women had comparatively little to do and spent a great deal of time in each other's houses, minding their children and exchanging the news of the last six months. In the evening, neighbours might drop by to discuss the day's hunting.

More than just a place for sleeping, the platform was the living room of the snowhouse. Warm and comfortable, it was where people ate and where guests were entertained, sitting along the edge of the platform as meat and ladles of soup were passed around. Here babies were nursed, small children curled up for a mid-day nap, puppies were played with, and stories were told. The platform was where people lived.

Directly opposite the middle of the platform was the entrance passage, which came into the house at the very bottom of the wall. The space between platform and entrance was used mainly as a cooking and food-processing area. Seals were butchered right on the snow floor. Furnishings consisted of a table made from a wooden board a little over a metre long and about a third as wide, supported by a strut braced against the floor and wall. Beside it was the lamp, supported on two stout sticks. Both lamp and table were arranged parallel to the front edge of the sleeping platform, leaving a wide enough gap for

the housewife to slide into her seat, handy for cooking.

The lamp was one of the most valuable items of personal property, used both for light and heat. Normally made of soapstone (a soft, talc-based rock found in a number of locations around Coronation Gulf and farther east in the Canadian Arctic), lamps were usually large and heavy, often a metre long or more, and in form like long, shallow, D-shaped saucers. The straight front edge supported the wick, made of cottongrass seeds or the fluffy "cotton" tufts of the same plant, soaked in oil and arranged in a row along the entire front edge. The rounded reservoir behind was filled with blubber that had been pounded or crushed to burst the vesicles of fat. Heat from the lamp flame slowly rendered the blubber into oil, allowing the lamp to feed itself. It was necessary, however, to tamp down the wick from time to time to keep it from smoking. Tending the lamp was one of the most symbolically important of a woman's tasks. In a household with two women, each would have her own lamp.

The cooking pot was also made of soapstone. In use it was suspended close above the lamp on sinew cords. Pots were usually rectangular with slightly flaring sides, perhaps 50 centimetres long, 20 centimetres wide, and 12 centimetres deep. Hung above this was the drying rack, a simple netted wooden container for drying mittens and other clothing overnight. In so small a house toilet facilities were obviously minimal. As a rule,

A wick made from a row of dried seeds was placed along the straight edge of the lamp. The raised platform along the curved edge functioned as a reservoir for extra blubber. The Copper Inuit were famous for their lamps, which in the 19th century were traded all the way to Alaska. This lamp is over a metre long.

Soapstone cooking pots were long and narrow, made to fit the area of the flame on a lamp. Boiling was essentially the only cooking technique used by Inuit.

Among the most symbolically important of a woman's tasks was the tending of the blubber lamp. In a household with more than one adult woman, each had her own lamp. By its light, she sewed clothing and looked after her children, while heat from the flame cooked the family's meals.

arrangements were made outdoors, although chamber pots were used at night or in bad weather.

Inevitably, the active social life of winter could not be contained within single-family snowhouses. A properly functioning winter village would always boast at least one dance house. A day or two after the snowhouses had been put up, someone, usually a person of respect and influence, would take the initiative and begin work on the dance house, constructing it around or as a kind of foyer to his own snowhouse. Friends and neighbours would stop by to help. A dance house could never stand alone. It had to be built in conjunction with a residential snowhouse, or better yet two linked houses, since that way it could be heated with their lamps.

The dance house was where all social happenings too large to fit into a single house took place. It was sometimes used for general visiting. Gymnastic performances were held here on long winter evenings. Most important of all, the dance house was the location of both drum dances and shamanic performances. It was the focus of the community.

A TREASURY OF TOOLS

Women made the clothing, but men made almost all the tools, including their wives' sewing equipment. This job was an important part of a man's duties, as self-sufficiency was much admired. Toolmaking was no easy task, for Inuit technology was perhaps the most elaborate and sophisticated of that of any aboriginal culture. This was less true in the Central Arctic than in Alaska or Greenland, but even the Copper Inuit had a tool for every imaginable task.

This Copper Inuit tool kit, extensive as it is, may be only a secondary kit, of the sort taken along on hunting trips.

Some of this technological sophistication may be due to the demands of the environment. The effective hunting of seals at their breathing holes, for instance, will inevitably require something more than just a club or a sharp stick. But traditional Inuit seem to have been in love with gadgetry, with the idea of having a tool for every purpose. They also had a keen appreciation of well-made objects and, in some areas, a fondness for decoration that make their tools among the most beautiful ever produced. The general qualities of a highly developed aesthetic sense, excellent workmanship, and overall technical complexity have characterized Inuit technology from its very beginning thousands of years ago. The Inuit toolmaking tradition demonstrates the capability of individual human beings in a time and place far from mass markets or craft specialization.

A number of tools were used simply for making other tools. Copper Inuit men kept two tool kits close at hand: a main kit, normally a skin bag or wooden box, and a smaller hunting kit attached to the bow case. The main kit might contain an adze, a home-made saw, a cutting board, antler wrenches or shaft-straighteners, splitting knives and wedges, gravers, whittling knives, and a bow-drill set. Some of these items might also find their way into the smaller hunting kit, normally reserved for tools specific to adjusting and repairing bows and arrows. Both kits would also hold spare parts and raw materials, such as coils of sinew, copper rivets and pins, spare arrowheads, useful chunks of antler, and broken or unfinished tool blanks. Men spent many a winter evening making and repairing tools.

Fishing lure made from a bear's tooth

Drill bearing or mouthpiece

Wound pin

Bow brace

Antler arrowhead

Iron blade

Marline spike

Graver

Shaft wrench

Man operating a bow drill. The loose bow string is looped around the drill, which is made to spin by sawing the bow back and forth. Downward pressure is maintained with a bearing held in the mouth, leaving the hands free. The bow drill was one of the most important traditional Inuit tools, and allowed the user to pierce almost any material.

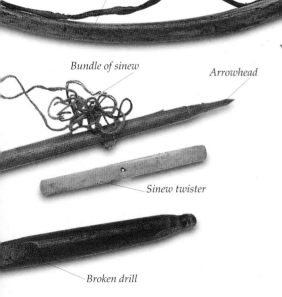

Drill

Drill bow

Bundle of sinew

Arrowhead

Sinew twister

Broken drill

Many of the tools used to fashion other tools had very deep roots in Inuit cultural history. One of the most useful was the bow drill, which consists of a small bow of wood or antler perhaps 40 or 50 centimetres long. The bow string was wrapped around a wooden drill shaft, and as the bow was pulled back and forth, the string caused the shaft to rotate. The bearing used to press down the top of the shaft was held in the mouth, leaving one hand free. The tip of the drill might be armed with a stone, bone, or metal bit. This tool gave Inuit craftsmen the ability to efficiently pierce even the hardest bone or ivory. In the absence of a saw, it could even be used for crosscutting, by drilling a line of holes and then hacking out the space between them.

But the bow drill was most useful for the role it played in making composite, multipart tools, many of which required strong but flexible joints. These were normally made by drilling a series of adjacent holes and then lashing the two parts together with sinew. This was the way to sew the skeleton of a kayak together, for instance, or to attach the "loose" fore-shaft of a throwing harpoon to the main wooden shaft. Other tools were more rigidly constructed, the different parts pegged in place, again through drilled holes. Without the bow drill,

Inuit technology would have been much simpler and less satisfactory.

Throughout the Central Arctic, caribou antler was the most important raw material for toolmaking. It is easy to find, relatively hard, and extremely flexible. After being steamed it can be bent into nearly any shape. Soaked in water for a few days, it becomes comparatively soft and easy to work, but then hardens up again after it dries.

In cross-section, antler has a hard outer cortex and a comparatively soft cancellous inner zone. Most toolmaking concentrated on the outer cortex. One of the most important techniques for working antler was the "groove-and-splinter" technique, whereby the craftsman incised a pair of long, parallel grooves on the antler using a short, strong blade. The grooves were angled towards each other at the bottom, and when deep enough, long strips of cortex could be levered out, which could then be used for arrowheads, knife handles, and a great range of other tools. Antler could also be cut in the round to make heavier, stronger tools like adze handles.

Musk-ox horn is even more plastic than antler, although much less hard. It was steamed and cut into shape to make ladles, drinking horns, hammers for pounding blubber, and the kind of ice scoop used by Copper Inuit in their breathing-hole seal hunting. Bows were sometimes made of musk-ox horn instead of wood. In Alaska, Dall sheep horn made a good substitute.

In Alaska and parts of the Eastern Arctic, ivory almost supplanted antler

as the basic raw material for making a great variety of objects such as harpoon heads, combs, and knife handles. It is a beautiful material, but extremely hard to work with simple tools. Like antler, though, it becomes somewhat easier to manipulate after a soaking in water or urine. Most Arctic ivory comes from walrus, although polar bear teeth were sometimes used for smaller items such as belt buckles or fish lures. In the Western Arctic, fossil mammoth ivory can sometimes be found eroding out from stream banks, usually in small pieces. It was occasionally employed in toolmaking, while in the East narwhal tusk had its own uses.

Wood did not enjoy as prominent a role in traditional Inuit technology as it did elsewhere in the world. Some Inuit lived almost entirely without wood, probably the only people on earth to do so. Wood-poor groups such as Netsilik and Polar Inuit used a variety of clever substitutes. Sleds might be made from polar bear hides, or even more ingeniously from fish wrapped in wet hides and frozen to make runners or cross-slats. Tent poles could be made of spliced antler, harpoon shafts from narwhal tusks, and bows from musk-ox horn. All these stratagems, however, had their price, and wood was certainly the preferred medium for many tasks.

Most Inuit did have access to wood, either driftwood or standing timber, but long trips were usually necessary to secure it. Almost always spruce, this wood was worked by splitting with a wedge, and by whittling and chopping. Saws came into use only after the Inuit acquired the necessary sheet metal.

The Inuit were excellent carpenters; because wood was often very precious, their task was almost more one of sculpting. They were excellent joiners, making large implements like sleds or kayaks out of many small pieces of wood carefully spliced, lashed, or pegged together. A strong, blood-based glue was often employed to further strengthen joints. Even items such as harpoon shafts or wooden boat paddles were commonly made from several pieces, because no single available piece of wood was

large enough. Objects fashioned from wood include boxes, snow goggles, bows, arrows, tables and cutting boards, tent poles, walking sticks, boat frames and paddles, sleds, bowls, snow shovels, spear and harpoon shafts, and various handles.

Bone had a limited usefulness because it is harder to work and more brittle than antler, although it does keep an edge better. Like antler, bone was commonly worked with the groove-and-splinter technique, to produce tiny sewing needles, along with larger bone arrowheads and long, narrow spoons used for scooping the marrow from long bones. Western Inuit made daggers from bear leg bones. Taking advantage of the hollow marrow cavity, the Copper Inuit made needlecases and drinking tubes from bird and caribou bone. Whale bone, by its very size and weight, recommended itself for use in the heaviest tools: pick or mattock heads, or even house support timbers.

Certain bones by their intrinsic shape suggest particular functions. One of the ankle bones of a caribou (the astralagus), for instance, was often used as the mouthpiece for a bow drill, since it is about the right size and has a ready-made socket on one side. The shoulder blade of a caribou or musk-ox was commonly used as a skin scraper, snow shovel, or for scaling fish.

Among the Copper Inuit, the only stone implements were lamps and cooking pots made of steatite. They were usually shaped right at the quarry with an adze, and were traded widely. Before the nineteenth century,

To obtain maximum flexibility, kayaks were lashed rather than pegged together wherever possible. Considering the wood resources available to most Inuit, the manufacture of a kayak was an extraordinary achievement. The frame was cut and spliced together from many small pieces of driftwood, and was usually covered with sealskin.

This man is using his teeth as a wrench to bend a wooden kayak rib into shape for mounting. Even the sophisticated tool kit of the Inuit had its limitations.

Western Inuit used pottery for the same purposes.

Most Inuit made knife blades and weapon tips from hard, glassy stone such as chert or flint, or flat-bedded stone like slate. The Copper Inuit used raw or native copper instead, which occurs in a nearly pure form at several locations in the Copper Inuit region. It was used for a considerable range of tools: sewing needles, adze blades, weapon tips, knife blades, ice picks, fish hooks, spear barbs, and various rivets and pins were all normally made of copper, where elsewhere bone, stone, or antler were the materials of choice. Copper was treated much like any other rock, and simply hammered cold into the

desired shape. All the raw materials mentioned thus far have been the direct local products of land and sea. One other, however, deserves mention: smelted iron. Before sustained European contact, iron was always very rare, and correspondingly precious. Traditional Inuit of five hundred or a thousand years ago lusted after iron the same way Europeans of that era coveted gold. Of the two metals, iron by far had the greater practical value.

The beauty of iron was its strength; it was harder than copper, less brittle than stone. Better than any other material, iron solved the main problem of Inuit technology: how to efficiently and easily work the hard organic materials such as antler and ivory from which most tools were made. Stone or copper would do in a pinch, but only iron was really strong enough. Long before enough iron was available for hunting knives or ulus, before there was enough for weapon points or cooking vessels, tiny pieces of iron were used in a thousand Arctic villages and camps to tip specialized knives used for cutting and splitting ivory and antler. Known as "composite knives," they had been developed specially to haft small iron blades less than two centimetres long in a handle strong enough for heavy work. With this knife and a bow drill, the Inuit craftsman was master of his materials.

MEN'S CLOTHING

Like his wife, a man wore two layers of clothing in cold weather — the inner layer with the fur side against his skin, the outer clothing (coat and trousers) hair-side-out. The winter clothing of an Inuit hunter served as his defensive armour against a frozen world. A man normally owned at least two sets of outer clothing: a rough, warm suit for mid-winter hunting or travelling, and a more stylish costume for less rigorous conditions.

This man is wearing a coat that combines the elaborate decoration of a formal coat with the warmer cut of a working coat, a compromise favoured by some eastern Copper Inuit.

Hair side worn toward the skin

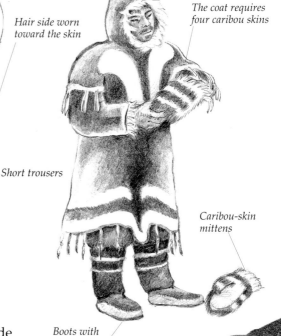

Hair side worn toward the skin

Short trousers

The coat requires four caribou skins

Caribou-skin mittens

Boots with nonslip soles

Among the Copper Inuit, the more formal, stylish coat was made from thin, late-summer hides, cut waist-high like the woman's coat except for a long narrow tail at the back reaching down to at least the knees. It closely resembled a modern dinner jacket, except that it was pulled on rather than buttoned down the front. The hood was small, much smaller than the woman's since it did not need to accommodate a baby. It was often made from caribou-head skins, the animal's ears, still attached, decorating the top. The shoulders were cut naturally, with none of the exaggerated bulkiness of a woman's coat, although the sleeves were awkwardly short by present-day standards. As with the woman's coat, inlaid white panels adorned the breast and inset bands of light-coloured hide encircled the arms.

The formal coat was not very warm. The high waist, rather short sleeves, and light material gave inadequate protection against the worst winter weather, particularly if the wearer was obliged to wait motionless beside a breathing-hole for hours at a time. Most men therefore owned

a second, plainer winter coat made from much heavier autumn hides. These working coats were cut straight around the bottom without the long tail of the dance coat, and reached almost to the knees, much longer than the formal coat.

Occasionally worn along with the rest of the more formal attire was a dance cap, made from coloured strips of short-haired caribou hide and loon skin, sewn together and surmounted at the top with a loon's bill. Usually owned only by the more influential men, but widely loaned out, dance caps were rarely worn except at dances (the hood otherwise protected the head).

In summer a man wore only a single layer of clothes, sometimes the outer dance coat, sometimes the inner coat. Most men also owned a waterproof summer jacket, roughly made from sealskins.

Men's trousers followed much the same style as women's. They were cut short, to about the knee, the outer pair decorated with inlaid horizontal strips of light-coloured hide and dyed de-haired hide. The caribou-hide stockings resembled loosely fitted

Made from thin August caribou hides, a man's formal or dance coat was not very warm, but it was elegantly cut and beautifully decorated.

Men wore short trousers coming to just below the knee. High boots covered the lower leg.

knee-high boots, overlapping the bottom edge of the trousers — thus quite different (and seemingly far more practical) than the "hip-waders" worn by women. Again, two layers were worn during the winter, and a pair of thick caribou-hide socks were worn between them. Over the stockings, low, ankle-high sealskin shoes were worn, so that the feet, the most vulnerable part of the body in cold weather, were encased in at least four layers of hide. Waterproof sealskin boots were often substituted in summer, and mittens were worn as needed.

Copper Inuit men often decorated the dance costume with lemming skins, and sometimes wore amulets. Three

kinds of amulets were recognized for men: those aimed at bringing success in the hunt, those meant to protect or strengthen various manly qualities, and those designed to establish a relationship with the supernatural. Whatever their function, most amulets consisted of parts of animals or other natural objects, usually sewed onto clothing. The more westerly Copper Inuit (including both Kahina's and Akuluk's people) were practically unique in the Inuit world for their lack of interest in amulets, a trait in keeping with an often agnostic attitude towards many aspects of the supernatural.

Amulets were more popular farther east, however, while Netsilik hunters sometimes wore so many they had to use a special belt to carry them all.

In the Western Arctic, men were sometimes tattooed. In contrast to women's tattooing, which was essentially decorative, Western Arctic men wore tattoos as a mark of courage or bravado. They usually took the form of oblique lines across the face or a cross on the shoulder, and marked the wearer as a successful whale hunter or, on occasion, a murderer to be feared (and admired). Labrets or lip plugs were also widely worn in the Western Arctic, normally as a pair worn under the corners of the mouth. The lower lip was usually pierced in adolescence, and the holes were gradually enlarged until they could accommodate a large labret. In the early nineteenth century, labrets decorated with a split Chinese blue bead were valued almost beyond price.

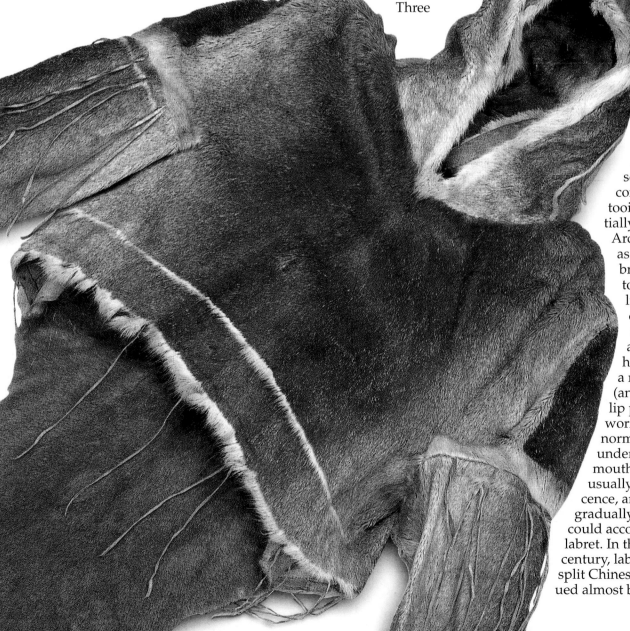

THE ANIMALS OF WINTER

Winter subsistence focused almost entirely on the single sea mammal dependably obtainable in the Central Arctic: the ringed seal. In a way, nature offered the Copper Inuit a choice.

The ringed seal is the common seal of the North American Arctic, found everywhere from western Alaska to eastern Greenland. The one seal that thrives under landfast ice, it was the basis of winter life in the Central Arctic.

Ringed seal

Harbour seal

Harp seal

Grey seal

Bearded seal

Hooded seal

One of the more widespread northern seals, the harbour seal lives in both the Atlantic and Pacific Oceans, from coastal California to the mouth of the Mackenzie River, and from northern Baffin Island to southern New England. Absent only from the Central Arctic, they were an important resource to many Inuit groups. They were hunted mainly on open water or from the edge of the fast ice, since they do not use breathing holes.

They could either hunt ringed seals on the sea ice, which they did, or devote their energies to hunting on land. Although most of the caribou have gone south by early winter, some choose to winter on the tundra, and small bands were available up the rivers flowing into Coronation Gulf from the south, or in the interior of Victoria Island. There were also musk-ox, scattered in small herds throughout the inland areas. The Inuit could have hunted both these animals, but did not.

There were several reasons why. Caribou and musk-ox move around a great deal and can be hard to find as well as difficult to hunt in winter. Inuit bow hunters depended on skill at stalking rather than any particular accuracy with their weapons. The winter snow is brittle and noisy to walk on, and animals are skittish and hard to approach. In addition, the interior is significantly colder than the coast because of the ocean's moderating effect.

But perhaps the most important reason has to do with the comparative leanness of caribou or musk-ox. Neither can produce the kind of fat that a seal can, fat the Inuit needed both for food and to fuel their lamps. The Copper Inuit knew other Inuit who lived so far from the sea coast that they were forced to live on caribou year-round. These were the so-called Caribou Inuit living around Akilinik and the Kazan River west of Hudson Bay. The Copper Inuit knew how much harder those lives were than their own. The Caribou Inuit starved more often, and lacking seal blubber for fuel, they were forced to burn bracken and willow outdoors all winter in even the worst weather (an open fire is, of course, impossible in a snowhouse). The Copper Inuit chose the comparative comfort of large villages on the sea ice and a steady diet of seal meat. Inland hunting was saved for the summer.

THE ICE SEAL

The ringed seal is the smallest of northern seals, and the most widespread, for it is at home in all Arctic waters. Perhaps more than any other single animal, it was the basis of Inuit

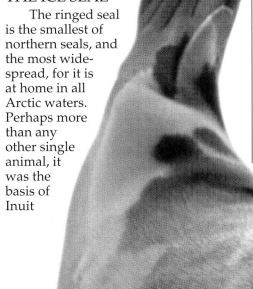

Arctic seals are all "true seals" (Phocidae). Unlike their relatives the earred seals (Otariidae), a group that includes sea lions, they cannot use their front flippers as legs, and have a great deal of trouble manoeuvring on land. The same is true of walrus.

subsistence from Alaska to Greenland. It was particularly important in the Central Arctic, since other sea mammals were absent. Secure beneath the winter ice, the ringed seal's only major enemy, besides man, was the polar bear.

The adult male, a little larger than the female, can weigh more than 90 kilos and measures up to a metre-and-a-half in length. The short, rather stiff coat is grey and lustrous — dark on the back and often marked with irregular creamy rings (hence the name), lighter on the belly. The pups are nearly white, born near the end of winter (between about 15 March and 15 April) in dens hollowed out under the sea ice. They are nursed by their mothers for about two months, learning to swim only as the sea ice begins to break up in mid-summer. Ringed seals reach sexual maturity at the age of six or seven years.

Ringed seals are the one sea mammal that actually seems to prefer land-fast ice in winter. In many parts of the Arctic fast ice is limited to bays and shore margins, with the moving pack ice lying beyond. Under these condi-

tions the larger, stronger animals live under the fast ice, forcing the younger, weaker seals out to the pack-ice zone. Fast ice offers better protection against

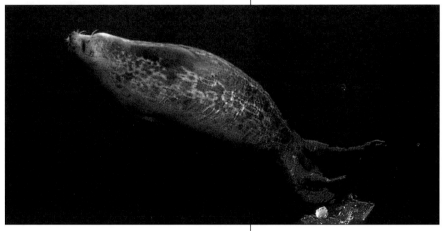

polar bears, and is needed by the adult females for denning.

Of course all seals living under landfast ice need to use breathing holes. Adult seals are normally rather solitary and territorial. Each has its own network of breathing holes, perhaps a dozen or so, which it must keep open by scratching and

By gnawing and scratching, ringed seals keep holes open through the sea ice for breathing during the winter, each animal maintaining perhaps a dozen holes. They give birth in ice dens in the spring.

The harp seal is a gregarious, migratory animal found only in the Eastern Arctic. In the spring, herds of harp seal follow the retreating pack ice from the waters off Newfoundland as far as Lancaster Sound and northwestern Greenland.

Polar bears give birth in the winter while the mother is in hibernation. Toward the end of November she digs a den in a snow bank on the side of a hill, or in a pressure ridge on the sea ice. She and her cubs do not emerge again until late March. Adult males hibernate for only a few weeks at mid-winter.

Polar bear liver is poison. It contains an enormous quantity of vitamin A, and if eaten can cause serious nausea, stomach cramps, temporary loss of sight, and sometimes even death.

gnawing at the ice. Once the ice has reached a certain thickness the seal is locked into this network, since its powers of excavation are limited. Exceptions occur where tidal cracks open to expose new areas of open water. As the crack freezes over, a seal can take advantage of the thin ice to move or shift its territory. In the Central Arctic, the ice is extremely stable, tidal cracks are rare, and seal populations tend to be quite sedentary throughout the winter.

Under good fast-ice conditions, populations have been estimated at between four and fourteen animals per square kilometre: far higher than the carrying-capacity of even the best interior tundra for caribou.

Awkward on land or ice, ringed seals are superb swimmers, able to dive to depths of a hundred metres and to stay submerged for periods of up to twenty minutes. Like all seals they are carnivores. In shallow water they eat mainly crabs, prawns, and fish such as polar cod and herring. In deeper water ringed seals feed directly on pelagic crustacean krill. Seals live intensively and eat little during the reproductive and nursing season, from April to late June. Their thick blubber layer is quickly reduced, from a maximum of about 40 percent of body weight to about 23 percent.

A BEARDED GIANT

Only one other species of seal frequents the waters of the Central Arctic: the bearded seal. This animal is much larger than a ringed seal, a mass of muscle and blubber weighing 400 kilos and nearly two-and-a-half metres long. In the

Copper Inuit territory bearded seals were most common in Dolphin and Union Strait, just northwest of Coronation Gulf, where tidal currents kept the winter ice quite thin. Bearded seals do not appreciate thick fast ice, although they can deal with it to some extent. If forced, they can keep breathing holes open through encroaching ice; they can also use the breathing holes of a ringed seal. Sometimes a hunter waiting at a breathing hole was surprised to harpoon one these monsters instead of the expected ringed seal.

Other important seal species are found outside the remote waters of the Central Arctic. There are two populations of harbour seals, one in Alaskan waters and the other living in the Eastern Arctic. Closely related is the harp seal of the Eastern Arctic, probably the best known of all northern seals because of its role in the controversial Newfoundland seal hunt. The hooded seal, another denizen of the Eastern Arctic, is as large as a bearded seal. The males sport an inflatable proboscis, and are very unusual-looking indeed. These Eastern and Western Arctic seals all need some open water for breathing.

A RESPECTED RIVAL

The Inuit consider polar bears as sea mammals, a sensible notion considering that they eat mainly seals and are rarely found far from the sea coast. The most carnivorous of bears, and the largest of all terrestrial carnivores, the polar bear is a formidable creature. Adult males average about 450 kilos, up to a maximum of 700 kilos, and can reach lengths of almost four metres. They can run faster than a man and are excellent swimmers. Polar bears have been sighted swimming in open water 40 kilometres from the nearest land.

The Inuit greatly respected bears for their strength and sagacity. Many Inuit seal-hunting techniques and tricks are said to have been learned from watching bears.

The Central Arctic is not the best place for a polar bear. The number of potential prey species is limited, and ice conditions are less than ideal for hunting. Polar bears prefer broken pack ice with some open water, which allows them to stalk seals basking on ice pans, or ambush them while swimming. Unfortunately this kind of ice is present for only a few weeks in most of the Central Arctic, primarily at break-up. The complete open water of late summer is a poor hunting ground, while winter fast ice is not much better. Polar bears are capable of waiting for seals at their breathing holes and killing them as they come up to breathe. But they are most numerous in areas where the ice better suits their requirements, particularly around the northern end of Hudson Bay and in the Eastern Arctic archipelago. In Copper Inuit territory polar bears were most abundant on the ice off the west coast of Victoria Island. Of all Copper Inuit, only the Kanghiryuarmiut of that area ate polar bear with any frequency.

Polar bears prey mainly on seals. Inuit elders often recount that they have learned many hunting tricks from watching bears.

Arctic foxes will follow polar bears and feed on their leftovers. Since a bear in good condition will often eat only the blubber of a seal, the pickings are sometimes very good.

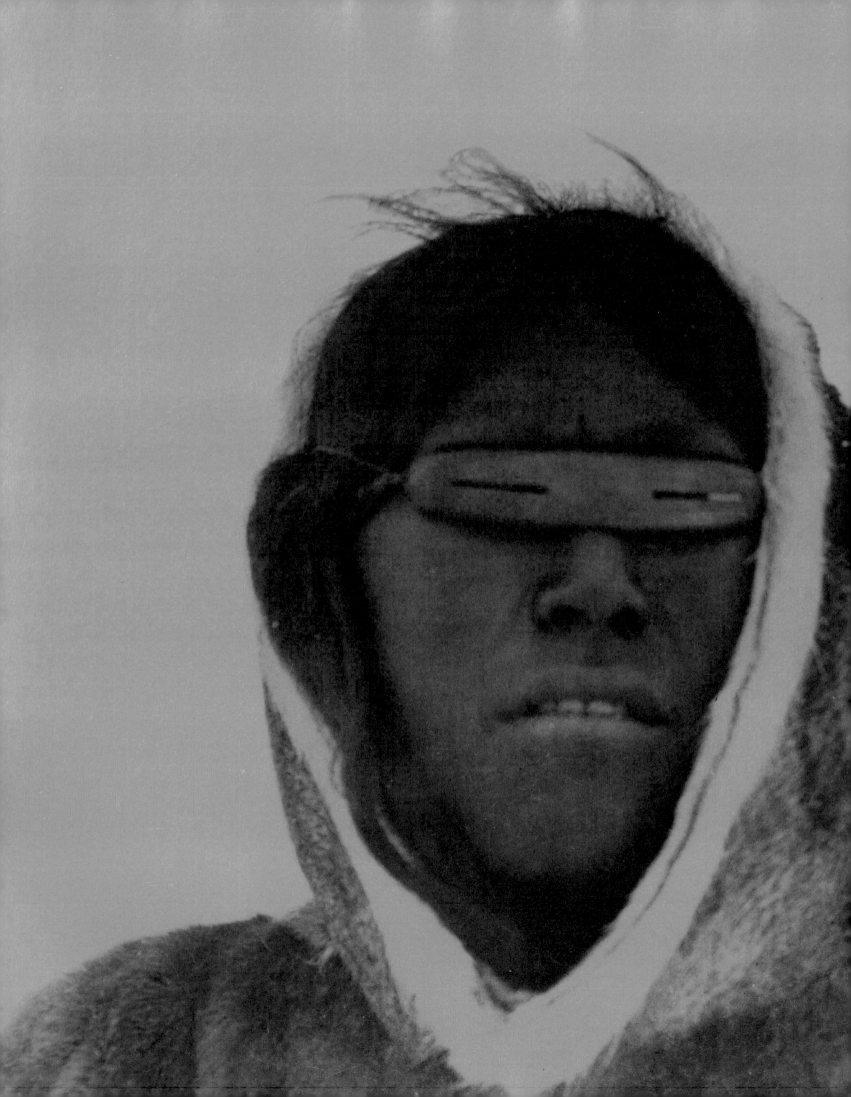

CHAPTER 4

THE SPIRIT OF THE BEAR

In spite of the mild weather, travelling was difficult. The dogs were sluggish after their long rest and the dazzling light was distracting. The blizzard had packed the snow into wild shapes, and the sled almost tipped several times. Akuluk stopped often to check on their direction.

Spring is the best time for travelling
— the days are long and the snow
still in good condition for sledding.
Because of the intense sunlight,
snow goggles are needed to
prevent eye damage.

As night fell on the second day, they arrived at Hanerak, where Akuluk knew many people and heard news of his family. He was impatient to get home now, so they started off again before dawn, having replenished their provisions with fresh meat.

That day, they saw the bear for the first time. It was walking very slowly, nose to the wind, moving away from the coast. Akuluk held back his dogs and they watched until it was lost from sight. Three white foxes were following the huge beast at a respectful distance. Akuluk believed he recognized his grandfather in this great white bear. The gait and the quiet strength — it must be him. He would wait for the bear: if his grandfather's soul was in it, it would come to him sooner or later.

Since they had left Noahognir, Akuluk had pushed his team as late as possible every day, leaving just a bit of light in the sky for making the snowhouse and settling down for the night. That day, he decided to set up camp in the middle of the day, and he built his snowhouse at the base of a steep bluff so that the bear wouldn't see or smell them. He then carefully lashed his heavy hunting knife to the end of his walking stick.

The next morning, Akuluk left the task of directing the sled almost entirely to Kahina. He walked

The bow and arrow was reintroduced to Arctic Canada by the Thule-culture ancestors of the modern Inuit. Because of poor quality wood, the Inuit bow derives its strength from a backing of braided caribou sinew.

beside her, searching the horizon with his eyes, seeking traces, signs on the ice, the voice of his grandfather in the wind. Then they saw the three foxes they had seen the day before. They seemed very lively, trotting proudly and snapping playfully at each other; they had obviously had a good meal. Soon the sled crossed the bear's tracks and, as they rounded a spur of rock, the bear came into view, walking toward the shore of a small bay, where, no doubt, it would sleep out in the sun. "My grandfather's soul is in him," Akuluk thought. "He is seeking peace."

Akuluk released his dogs as soon as he was certain the bear had noticed their presence. He was worried that Kaumaq in particular would be hurt. Agluak knew the danger — this was not the first bear he had faced — but Kaumaq was jumping around and getting too close. Still, Akuluk knew that the dogs would keep it busy. He could take his time.

He advanced slowly, holding his weapon high, careful not to make noise, even though the bear could see him perfectly. It came toward him, sent by his grandfather's soul, and raised itself up on its hind legs to receive his makeshift spear full in the heart. And it remained upright, groaning, batting at the air with its enormous paws, trying to reach Akuluk. The dogs bayed and growled, darting in and out as they harried the huge animal. Kahina, frightened, stayed beside the sled.

Akuluk managed to pull his spear from the bear's chest and thrust it into the heart again, deeper, two or three times. The bear fell to the ice. Akuluk stood over it and watched it die. The dogs, suddenly quiet, lay down and watched too. In the bear's eyes, Akuluk saw the soul of his grandfather, slipping away. He pulled his harpoon out and stuck it in the snow so that the point was straight up in the air. The soul was still clinging to it, and would stay there for several days.

Kahina and Akuluk offered the bear a small bow and arrow as a token of their thanks, then they skinned it. The three foxes watched from a distance. As soon as the humans moved off, they would close in. Once more the bear would provide them with a meal.

Their task finished, Akuluk and Kahina started walking again, silently, pensively. Akuluk was tired and the dogs were moving slowly. The sled was now very heavily loaded, for the bear skin and much of the meat had been added. In two or

three days, they would be at Kanghiryuak and Akuluk did not want to depend on his family for food.

One evening, they passed a cape flanked with islands against which the blizzard had massed snowdrifts. Soon after, they saw tracks of a sled, wider than theirs by a good hand, and then other tracks, and in a little while they were within sight of the village. As soon as they were noticed there was an explosion of shouts and laughter. All the Kanghiryuarmiut came out into the night to meet them and everyone hugged everyone else.

The Noahognirmiut liked to laugh, Kahina thought, but nothing like the Kanghiryuarmiut. That evening, they practically laughed till they cried. Akuluk and his friends exchanged great affectionate punches. The dog Agluak, finding his friends after a year away, was so excited that he had to be tethered at a distance. Kahina, at first a little intimidated, finally let herself be carried away on the waves of laughter.

Over the next few days, Akuluk let Kahina relate the adventures of their journey so that she would be known and liked by his family and friends. She slid painlessly into her new life, happy and serene. At first, she remembered her trip to Kanghiryuak as being very long, but as time passed, it seemed much shorter. Sometimes, she wondered if it had all been a dream, like the famine when she was a child.

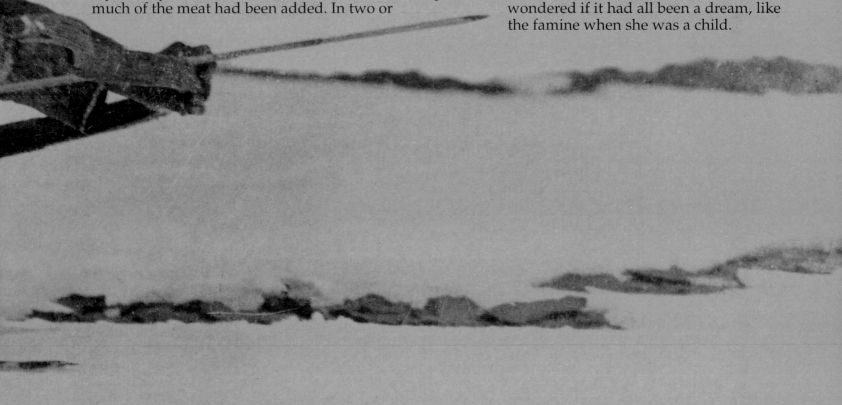

THE FRIEND OF MAN

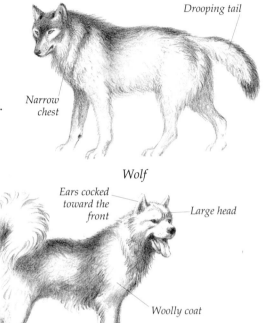

The Inuit believed that the bond between people and dogs was an ancient one. After all, part of the human race was fathered by a dog, and they occupied such an important place in Inuit culture that it is difficult to see how people could have lived without them. Dogs were mankind's only real ally in the animal world.

In traditional times, few Copper Inuit families could afford to keep more than two dogs. The popular image of Inuit driving dogsleds as we now drive cars dates to a later period. With only two dogs you do not sit on the sled; you get off and help pull.

People were not always particularly kind to their dogs, and sometimes beat them, even brutally. Arctic archaeological sites dating back many hundreds of years have produced dog skulls with compressed fractures on the forehead, suggesting that this attitude is not new. To be fair, however, driving dogs can be an unusually difficult and frustrating task. Most sled dogs are inveterate fighters, forever quarrelling and getting their traces tangled. After a particularly exhausting sled journey, one early Anglican missionary wrote that he could not believe that a just God would punish a man for cursing or beating his dogs.

Although sometimes harshly treated, dogs were still part of the family. And the Copper Inuit were more gentle toward their dogs than were most. Perhaps having so few they valued them more. Beatings were comparatively rare, and in the winter the dogs were allowed to sleep in the entrance tunnel, rather than outside as was the rule elsewhere. Bitches with pups were even permitted to sleep in the house. When camp was moved,

Snow goggles work by restricting the field of vision to a mere slit, thus reducing the amount of light reaching the optic nerve. They were commonly made of wood, antler, or ivory.

Drooping tail

Narrow chest

Wolf

Ears cocked toward the front

Large head

Woolly coat

Greenland Dog

All Arctic dogs share a general family resemblance. The breadth of their chest and a tail that curls up over the back distinguish them from their distant ancestor, the wolf. Their division into distinct, recognized breeds is a very recent phenomenon, reflecting in part the interests of modern dog breeders intent on saving Arctic blood lines from genetic swamping.

As long as the seal hunting was good during the winter, dogs were generally well fed, and often went for weeks without having to pull a sled. Their only daily task was to help with the seal hunting.

Full tail

Light-coloured coat

Thick ruff

Samoyed

Mask

Black nose

Black, white, and silver coat

Qimmiq

Multicoloured coat

Double coat

Alaskan malemute

women or girls sometimes kept tiny pups warm by carrying them in their coat hoods.

The Copper Inuit went so far as to name puppies after a recently deceased relative (no disrespect was intended). As well, a newborn pup, like a newborn child, was massaged or handled in a kind of ritual designed to bestow certain qualities on it. A pup's legs were pulled to make them grow strong, and its tail twisted to curve over the back. Its nostrils might be pierced with a pin to give it a good sense of smell, while an arrow rubbed along the belly would make it swift in pursuit. The pup might be tied in a miniature harness so it would pull well, or a weight placed on its back to enable it to carry a summer pack with ease. All the while its owner would exhort it to grow large and be strong.

Dogs had many duties. In winter they pulled the sled; in summer they became pack animals, lugging 15 or 20 kilos of baggage. They also helped with the hunting, harassing polar bears and sniffing out seals' breathing holes. Their barking protected the camp from bears, or strangers.

In winter the dogs would be called into the house and given any dinner leftovers as well as strips of lamp blubber from which most of the

Summer was a difficult season for dogs, who were often poorly nourished and expected to work hard carrying heavy packs.

oil had been consumed. In times of plenty they also got meat and guts, and occasionally sealskins with some of the blubber still attached. If times were hard, they were the first to do without. As one man explained, "Dogs are more used than men to going without food. They can stand it better, and anyway we have the upper hand."

Dogs usually fared more poorly in summer. This was the time of year when fishing was important, and dogs were often fed on little more than scraps and broth made from bones. They did more work in summer too, hauling packs almost every day; in winter they might not be run for weeks at a time. Not surprisingly, most dogs tended to be very gaunt by the end of summer.

The Inuit favoured the reproduction of useful, handsome animals. Bright eyes, a good coat, and a strong tail curving sharply over the back were all much admired. With time, and some inevitable genetic isolation from dogs living elsewhere in the world, there developed a particular race or family of dogs living across the Arctic from Siberia to Greenland, known to modern breeders as the spitz family, but popularly called huskies. Within it a number of geographic variants or breeds are recognized, including the blue-eyed Siberian husky, the white samoyed, the powerful Alaskan malemute, the qimmiq or Canadian Inuit sled dog, and the Greenland dog. All share a similar compact body, wedge-shaped head with upright ears, and curly tail. Males usually run about 35 or 40 kilos, with females significantly smaller. The pups are generally precocious, and attain sexual maturity earlier than most other dogs. But contrary to popular legend, Inuit dogs are not half wolf. All dogs are ultimately descended from wolves, but that origin lies in the distant past.

THE ENDLESS WAIT

The men left at daybreak to hunt seal on the sea ice. They walked for a good hour, chatting. As they approached the hunting area, they lowered their voices and began to spread out a little, each holding his dog on a leash, his weapon in hand, his tool kit on his back.

The air was filled with the crunch of boots on snow, the sparkling of stars in the lightening sky. Soon, each man heard only his own breath, his own heart beating in the immense blue space, his dog's panting as it searched in the tangled winds that blew along the sea ice for the intoxicating scent of seal.

In the bays and gulfs of the Central Arctic, the ice rarely moves all winter, and by April, breathing holes may have to penetrate two metres deep. Conical in cross-section, they narrow at the top to an apex only a few centimetres in diameter, buried under half a metre of snow.

This snow is actually an advantage to the seal, since it is easy to breathe through and offers some protection from both cold and predators. From the surface, snow-covered breathing holes can be completely invisible. The Copper Inuit hunter had to solve two problems: how to find an active hole in the first place, and how to know when the seal was coming up to breathe. He had somehow to get his harpoon into an animal he could not even see.

The seal is an intelligent and quick-witted animal. It will not use any hole where the snow has been visibly disturbed. Nor will it come up if it smells anything amiss. Shuffling feet on the snow overhead, a cough — all were sufficient to scare it away.

To find the hole, the hunter examined and probed every suspicious mound. But usually it was the keen sense of smell of the hunter's dog that succeeded. For although the hole was nearly invisible, nothing could mask the warm, rich smell of seal.

Once the breathing hole had been discovered, the hunter probed it with his long antler "feeler" until he found its exact shape and centre. He then carefully stamped the snow around the probe and drew it out, leaving only a deep hole about a centimetre in diameter. Down this he pushed his

indicator, a narrow stick of antler as thick as but twice as long as an ordinary steel knitting needle. The indicator was tied to a small anchor stuck in the snow outside the hole, which kept it in place.

The dog was now staked up where it could not cause trouble or make a noise that might scare the seal. The hunter might cut a block of snow for a seat, or build a low windbreak if he anticipated a long wait. He placed his feet on

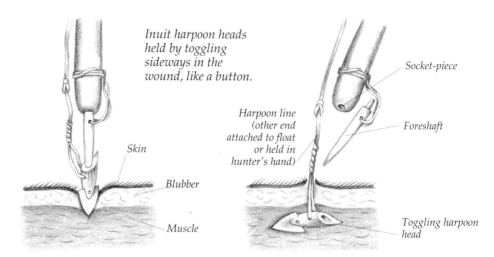

Inuit harpoon heads held by toggling sideways in the wound, like a button.

Skin

Blubber

Muscle

Harpoon line (other end attached to float or held in hunter's hand)

Socket-piece

Foreshaft

Toggling harpoon head

Most hunting required the ability to wait for long periods in often cold and uncomfortable weather. This man is jigging for fish through the ice, peering down into the dark water waiting for a strike.

Antler head

Raw copper rivet

Braided sinew harpoon line

Iron endblade

The Copper Inuit used harpoons only for hunting seals on the ice.

a pad of bear skin to keep them from freezing and arranged his harpoon ready for use before him on a pair of wooden supports. He then remained perfectly still. Every few minutes he stooped down to check the indicator, then lifted his head to scan the horizon.

The Inuit breathing-hole harpoon was a little shorter than the man carrying it. It had a detachable and very sharp head. To it was attached a braided sinew line, the other end of which the hunter grasped in his left hand as he struck with his right. Below the head, the wood-and-antler composite shaft was light and fairly rigid, well adapted for stabbing down a narrow breathing hole.

Formidable patience was required to wait for a seal. It meant complete, unmoving silence for hours, even days, at temperatures as low -40° or -45° C. And it meant total concentration, since the hunter had only the briefest warning, the most fleeting instant to strike. The hunter's reflexes had to be sharper than his harpoon blade.

CAPTURING THE SEAL

At last the seal visited that one particular hole. As it came up to breathe, its nose touched the end of the indicator, causing it to rise slightly and quiver. This warned the hunter, who stood with uplifted harpoon and struck with all his might as the indicator dropped.

Unless the point of the harpoon actually pierced its skull, the seal was not usually killed outright. In fact, sometimes the hunter missed altogether, since his target was a spot no more than a very few centimetres in diameter. If he struck successfully, a struggle ensued. He had to hold the thrashing, fighting seal on the end of the harpoon line with his left hand — and a ringed seal is a relatively large, strong animal — while with his right hand he dug out the breathing hole using a horn scoop and the ice pick at the butt end of the harpoon. When the hole was big enough, he pulled the seal up onto the ice and killed it, either by stabbing it through the eye or crushing its fragile skull.

Should his prey turn out to be a great bearded seal the hunter might find himself in some trouble. Few men were strong enough to hold this animal, although some lost fingers trying. Usually the hunter was forced to call for help.

A ringed seal belonged to the man who killed it, although it would later be shared out according to complex formal rules. But by tradition a bearded seal belonged to everyone within sight or sound at the time of its capture. When a hunter called out for help, everyone came running.

A strong attitude of masculine bravado developed around the sharing out of a bearded seal. Each man hacked away wildly with his knife in a kind of frenzy, often giving and receiving terrible cuts. A man could not hang back and appear timid. Fortunately, perhaps, it was uncommon to kill a bearded seal. After killing a ringed seal it was only necessary to pour a little water in the seal's mouth as an offering.

All the active men of a village would normally go out hunting together in the morning, fanning out over an area of several square kilometres once the sealing grounds were

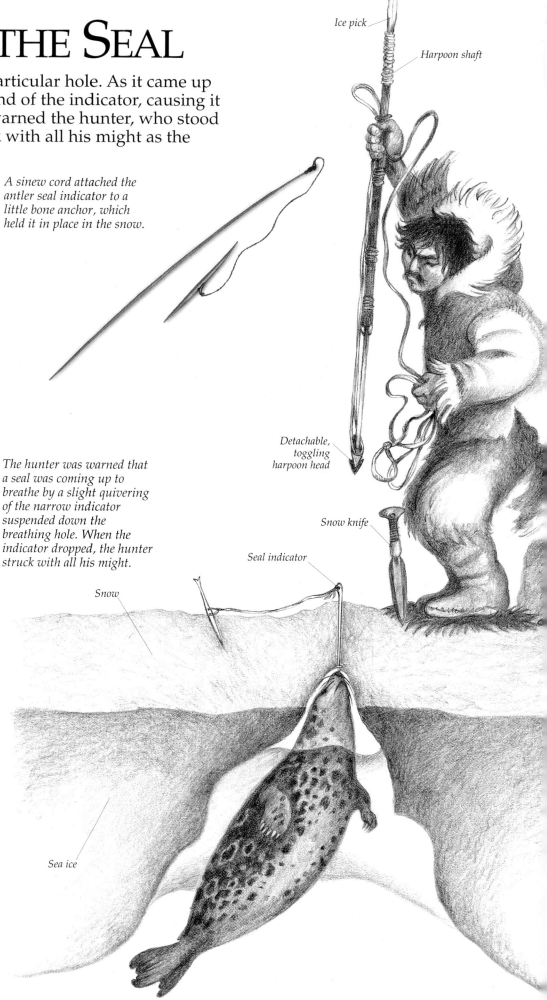

A sinew cord attached the antler seal indicator to a little bone anchor, which held it in place in the snow.

The hunter was warned that a seal was coming up to breathe by a slight quivering of the narrow indicator suspended down the breathing hole. When the indicator dropped, the hunter struck with all his might.

Ice pick

Harpoon shaft

Detachable, toggling harpoon head

Snow knife

Seal indicator

Snow

Sea ice

Shaft

Socket-piece

Harpoon line

Foreshaft

Toggling
harpoon head

The harpoon used for stabbing down a breathing hole was not a very imposing weapon. The prey was relatively small and there was little danger of breakage, since after the head had detached the shaft was still held in the hunter's hand.

Ice scoop

Snow block
for seat

reached. Should someone make a kill early in the day, he would probably decide to continue hunting at another hole rather than return home early. In a typical successful day, a party of fifteen men might kill three or four seals.

Just as the men left as a group in the morning, they came home together at the end of the day, whatever seals they had killed. Back in the village a sharp lookout was kept, and they would be met partway out by a party of women and children. The boys jumped on the dead seals and pretended to kill them with their toy harpoons, thereby bringing good luck to their fathers. The dogs knew their own houses and brought the seal right up to the door.

The rigorous conditions of winter hunting began to relax in early May, with longer and warmer days. In spring both ringed and bearded seals will often haul themselves out onto the ice to bask in the sun. In some areas it is not uncommon to see as many as a dozen animals on the ice at a time. This created an opportunity for the skilled hunter, who could stalk a seal and try to harpoon it before it could escape down its hole.

The task sounds easier than it was. There is no cover on the spring ice, and a basking seal is constantly on the lookout for predators, sleeping for only a few seconds at a time. It sleeps right beside its hole, ready to slip down with the least twitch. To calm the seal the hunter had to pretend to be a seal himself. He would lie on his side, hands hidden, moving

one leg up and down in imitation of a seal waving its hind flippers and scratching at the ice. When his intended prey was asleep, he would crawl rapidly toward it, headfirst so that his progress was less obvious, elbows and knees working furiously through any pools of water in the way. When the seal raised its head to look around, the hunter would stop and resume his pretense.

If all went well, he could over the course of perhaps an hour get within ten paces or so of the animal. He would then make a dash for it, and attempt to get his harpoon into the seal before it could dive down its hole. Much depended on the element of surprise. Whether successful or not, the hunter always managed to get totally soaked and chilled to the bone.

In spring it was sometimes practical to involve the women and children in a seal hunt. Often a kind of party mood reigned, with everyone joking and kidding in the warm air. By now the breathing holes had melted open and were easy to spot. Everyone would take a hole. If the seal came up at one guarded by a woman or child, that person would cry out "I see it, I see it," and bang on the ice with a stick to scare the seal down again before it had the chance to breathe. With all of its holes being watched, the seal was eventually forced to surface at a hole guarded by a hunter, where it would be captured.

Spring sealing was little practised by the Copper Inuit, who mostly preferred to be inland fishing somewhere by the last half of May. Their Netsilik neighbours, however, were masters at this type of hunting, and depended on it to lay up a store of blubber for the seasons to come.

WAR AND JUSTICE

Warfare was rare among most Inuit. Where it did occur, it was limited to a quick surprise attack by a handful of warriors. The object was to catch the enemy unprepared, and then kill everyone.

Warfare like this, widespread enough among Indian groups to the south, was found only among the more politically structured Inuit groups. In Alaska and the Mackenzie Delta area, for instance, each of the various Inuit societies controlled a well-defined territory and existed in a state of near-permanent hostility with its neighbours. Here warfare was relatively common, both between different Inuit groups and between Inuit and Indians.

By contrast, the Inuit of the Central Arctic — the Netsilik, Iglulik, Caribou, and Copper Inuit — were almost totally igno-rant of war. It is not that they were pacifists or less belligerent than their coun-trymen in the West, but only that they did not have the social organization or institutions, or even sufficient population density, to give warfare any real meaning.

As well as knives, hunting weapons such as bows and lances were used in fighting.

A FEAR OF STRANGERS

The Copper Inuit were probably never threatened by violent invasion. There were occasional raids by Chipewyan and Yellowknife Indians living to the south, but these seem to have been motivated by a desire for revenge and glory rather than conquest. These groups often blamed Inuit magic for mysterious deaths or other misfor-tunes, and there existed an ancient tra-dition of mutual suspicion and hatred between the two races.

Raids seem to have been fairly infrequent, and there is no record that the Copper Inuit were ever the aggres-sors. There are traditional stories of Inuit attacking Indians they met by chance, but they seem to have tried as much as possible to avoid them. Inuit, for example, sometimes made trips down to the area just north of Great Bear Lake to obtain wood. Here on the fringe of the forest a very sharp lookout was kept for any sign of Indians: old camp sites, smoke from fires, and so on.

Even the appearance of strange Inuit was something to be dealt with cautiously. In Inuit tradition strangers were generally dangerous and deceit-ful; the more strange, the more distant their homeland, the more they were not to be trusted. As one Copper Inuit song put it:

*I have been told of people west of us
I have been told of the people west of us,
With their big knives, and their big arrows,
I am afraid.*

When strangers were first sighted, the immediate reac-tion was to flee.

Alternatively, the women and children hid while the men formed a line, weapons in hand. They then advanced upon the strangers. An emissary was sent, sometimes a child, to discover the strangers' intentions. If they were friendly, tensions relaxed. After intro-ductions there was often a wrestling match between some of the younger men to "break the ice." Afterwards the two groups would eat together, and a dance would be held that night. Individuals and families would estab-lish formal dance or even spouse-exchange partnerships to further cement relations. Certainly the fact that Inuit shared a common language made it relatively easy to keep the peace if both groups desired it.

Dealings with whites could be dif-ficult, especially in the early days before relations were well established. Several traditional Copper Inuit stories describe white attacks on Inuit camps. Although none of these attacks has been recorded in any written histories, they nonetheless betray considerable uneasiness on the part of the Inuit toward white newcomers. Yet in the long run whites were found to be generally friendly.

In the Western Arctic many Inuit were a good deal more bellicose than their eastern relatives, not only towards each other but towards strangers as well. For instance, when John Franklin came down the Coppermine River on his first expedition in 1821, the local Copper Inuit fled before him, mistaking the party for Indians. Five years later on his second expedition to the Arctic, Franklin encountered a very different reception on his trip down the Mackenzie River. He and his party were besieged by a fleet of Mackenzie Inuit kayakers, and nearly overwhelmed. Only through considerable forbearance was bloodshed avoided.

MURDEROUS PASSIONS

Warfare takes place between groups of comparative strangers. Particularly in the Central Arctic, violence was usually more solitary, more intimate: murder, in other words. Despite the popular image of the Inuit as a particularly friendly, smiling people, murder was distressingly common. In the early 1920s the traveller Knud Rasmussen talked with a village of fifteen Copper Inuit families near Bathurst Inlet. All of the men had been involved in a killing in one way or another.

Motives, of course, varied, but perhaps the most common was competition over women. As we shall see, most Copper Inuit were unable, because of difficult circumstances, to raise more than a fraction of their newborn baby girls. As a result, there were not enough women of marriageable age to go around. Given the necessity of acquiring a wife by one means or another, it is not surprising that violence often ensued.

Anger and jealousy also figured as common motives. In one story, a Copper Inuit man was sitting in his tent sharpening a knife he had just made. A neighbour entered and began to jeer at him, saying he had no idea how to make a knife. The owner quietly contin-

This Alaskan Inuit fishing line sinker is decorated with an incised scene showing a surprise attack on a village.

Meat rack

The dog who didn't bark and warn his masters

Archer

Attackers

Someone (attackers? defenders?) closing the door of the house

Attackers

ued to sharpen his weapon until its edge was keen enough. He then drove the knife into the jester's stomach with the remark, "Now see if I can't make a knife."

The ideal of vengeance was well entrenched. One of Rasmussen's murderers was a twelve-year-old boy who shot his own father because he was cruel to the boy's mother. There was an obligation to avenge close relatives, and murder often led to murder.

THE INDIVIDUAL AND SOCIETY

As stories like these illustrate, with respect to violence the Copper Inuit lived essentially without law, as we would understand the term now. There were acknowledged rules of behaviour, but no way to enforce them beyond private vengeance and self-defense. Without police, army, courts, and jails, one had to rely on one's own strength and the help of kin and friends. Thus the high murder rate, since every man had to look after his own interests, and punishment did not follow automatically. Murder was not even the subject of serious social disapproval. Many of the most respected men in the community were, by our standards at least, murderers.

For other crimes, however, public opinion could be a potent force. In fact, dishonesty, laziness, stinginess, and bossiness were more likely to damage a person's reputation than a violent killing. The overbearing, pushy man, the niggardly wife who shared only the most meagre cuts of meat, the lazy hunter — all would quickly become objects of public ridicule and humiliation. In the intimacy of a small, closed community, the sarcasm and laughter of others could be extremely wounding. What else is there to live for, really, besides the esteem and respect of one's fellows?

Nor were there many secrets. Theft, for instance, was very rare, not only because there was little to steal, but even more because there was no chance of getting away with it. Everyone knew that this was Kunana's knife, that was Kallak's sled. The thief would be immediately caught and denounced. Of course to take from people outside the group was not really theft at all, but rather something to brag about, the besting of a stranger. The social contract did not include outsiders.

The difference seems to have been that murder and other crimes of violence were normally matters between individuals. Offenses such as stinginess and bossiness were social crimes, affecting everyone and violating the social life of the group. Only when violence got out of hand did it become a group concern.

SYSTEMS OF JUSTICE

The absence of real leadership roles may have seriously limited the ability of the Copper Inuit to deal with problems of violence, since there was no authority figure to protect the weak or see that justice was done. Other Inuit had whaling captains (*umialiq*) or camp bosses (*issumataq*), men who exercised authority and sometimes real power. These were not hereditary positions. Inuit leaders were listened to and obeyed because of their abilities and wisdom, because they kept the group prosperous and at peace with itself. It was not usually in their interest to allow serious violence within the group, and they would do everything they could to stop it.

One of the most elaborate examples of an Inuit justice system comes from the southern coast of Baffin Island. Here a court was called to determine the guilt or innocence of the accused; if guilty, they were sentenced by a conclave of powerful chiefs. Punishments extended to banishment and death, and were not themselves to be the subjects of subsequent vengeance. In other words, they were socially sanctioned. The court met regularly in a traditional location, and continued in operation until the arrival of the RCMP in the 1920s.

Even among the Copper Inuit, there were well-respected men who might bring their influence to bear on issues of justice and

The butt of this ivory whip handle is carved in the shape of a clenched fist.

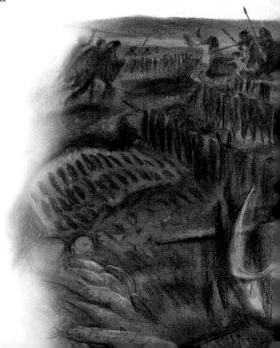

80

revenge. In 1915-16 the pioneer ethnologist Diamond Jenness spent many months living with Copper Inuit around southwestern Victoria Island. During that time he was accused of murdering a man through sorcery. It was a serious charge, and if widely believed he might easily have been killed by the murdered man's kin.

Several of Jenness's friends appealed to Uloksak, a respected local shaman. Uloksak staged a public shamanic performance, with the avowed purpose of discovering through spiritual means whether or not Jenness was guilty. A good showman, he pretended to be able to speak English, or more accurately to be in the possession of an English-speaking spirit. Jenness played along and the audience was convinced of Uloksak's abilities. With the help of his spirits, the shaman was able to conclude that it had been another *qablunaq* who lived far away, not Jenness, who was responsible for the death. A crisis was averted. Whether or not Uloksak's behaviour was influenced by the fact that he depended on Jenness and his expedition to obtain ammunition for a newly purchased rifle is uncertain.

The first European to visit the Copper Inuit was Samuel Hearne. Early one July morning in 1771, his Chipewyan and Yellowknife Indian guides fell upon an Inuit fishing camp at Bloody Falls on the lower Coppermine River, killing all 21 inhabitants. Hearne's account — faithfully depicted here — may have been sensationalized by his publisher to spur sales.

CHAPTER 5

THE FAMILY OF AKULUK AND KAHINA

During their long trip from Noahognir, Akuluk had told Kahina many stories about the people of Kanghiryuak, so that by the time they arrived, she felt as though she knew almost everyone, even the dead people and the dogs. She recognized practically all of them: this man by his loud, cheerful voice, that man by his arrogance, this woman who liked to flirt, that one who had a sharp tongue.

The anthropologist Diamond Jenness was one of the pioneers of "participant observation" as a means of learning about another culture. He recorded much of what we now know about how the Copper Inuit lived in the days before the fur trade.

Kahina also knew who was the best seamstress, who was the worst hunter, who was the best dancer, who would become a shaman, who was jealous of whom, who was in love with whom.

As they travelled, her husband had told her so much about hunting and fishing with his brother Tavlo and the arguments they had had when they were children that she knew him as well as she knew her cousins. And she understood that Tavlo was more than a brother; he was a friend, the hunting partner with whom Akuluk shared everything.

Tavlo's wife, Nik, was young and shy, but very gentle and nice, just as Akuluk had described her. He hadn't known, however, that she had had a baby at the end of the summer, while the Kanghiryuarmiut were in the tundra — a big fat-cheeked boy, Kunana, whom she still kept under her coat almost all the time.

The only person whom Kahina didn't recognize right away was Akuluk's father. She was expecting a big hunter, vigorous, full of life and strength and authority, but she was introduced to an old man with trembling hands, sad and clouded eyes, a broken voice. She was shocked at Akuluk's indifference toward this old man, about whom he had spoken with such warmth and respect. He didn't even speak to him and never listened to him, as if he

Whenever possible, the Copper Inuit built their food and equipment caches on off-shore islands or along cliff edges as a protection against predators. Like most Inuit they depended a great deal upon stored provisions during certain seasons of the year.

were angry at him for no longer being the strong man who had once commanded everyone's admiration.

Akuluk built his snowhouse right beside Tavlo's, using the same access tunnel and making a common vestibule. This space soon became a meeting place for men on their way from the hunt and for women to come and gossip during the day, sitting or lying down together, wrapped in caribou blankets. And the children came and went, played, laughed, and cried. From time to time, Nik took her baby out from under her coat and everyone played with him and caressed him. Agara, who had lost her own baby, sometimes nursed him.

It was the same life as in Noahognir, Kahina thought; the same heavy, warm smells, the same flickering lamplight, the same sleepiness that overcame them in the middle of the day. While they waited for the men to come home from the hunt, they talked about everything under the sun, dreamed a little, repaired clothes, made oil for the lamps, melted some ice and boiled the meat. And the next day, they did the same thing again.

Unless a blizzard was blowing, the men went out to hunt before dawn and came home after night had fallen. In the morning, Kahina always woke up at the same time as Akuluk. Without leaving the sleeping platform, she would feel her way to the lamp and light it, as Nik lit hers, and the igloos would warm gently while the men were eating

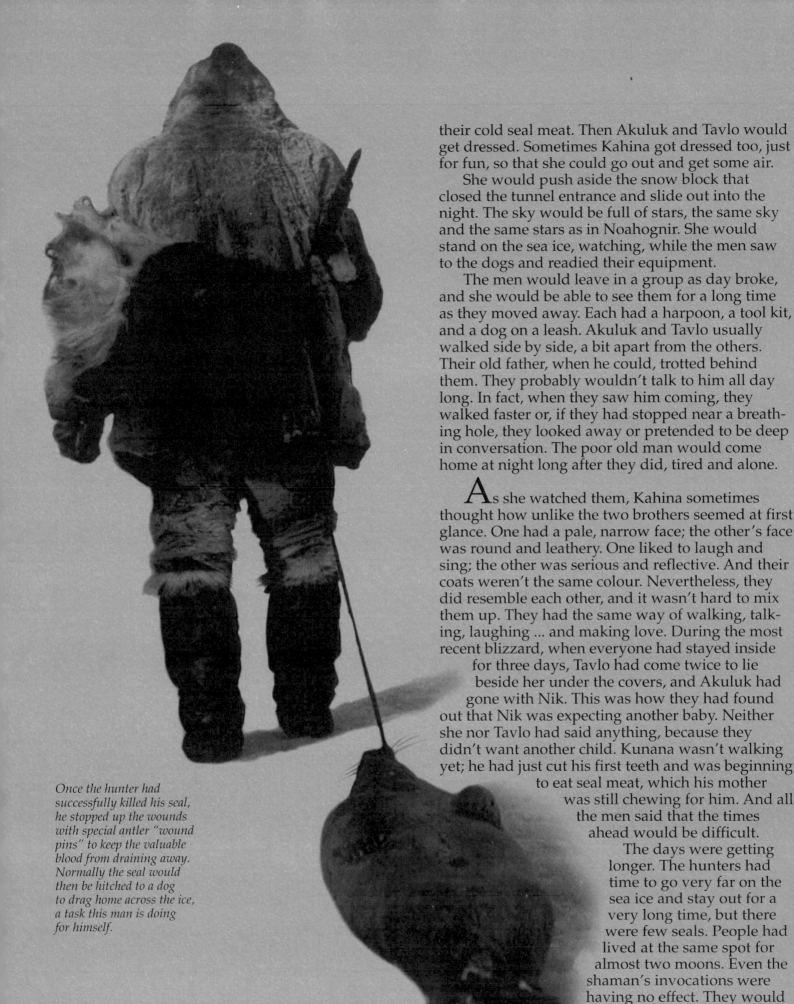

Once the hunter had successfully killed his seal, he stopped up the wounds with special antler "wound pins" to keep the valuable blood from draining away. Normally the seal would then be hitched to a dog to drag home across the ice, a task this man is doing for himself.

their cold seal meat. Then Akuluk and Tavlo would get dressed. Sometimes Kahina got dressed too, just for fun, so that she could go out and get some air.

She would push aside the snow block that closed the tunnel entrance and slide out into the night. The sky would be full of stars, the same sky and the same stars as in Noahognir. She would stand on the sea ice, watching, while the men saw to the dogs and readied their equipment.

The men would leave in a group as day broke, and she would be able to see them for a long time as they moved away. Each had a harpoon, a tool kit, and a dog on a leash. Akuluk and Tavlo usually walked side by side, a bit apart from the others. Their old father, when he could, trotted behind them. They probably wouldn't talk to him all day long. In fact, when they saw him coming, they walked faster or, if they had stopped near a breathing hole, they looked away or pretended to be deep in conversation. The poor old man would come home at night long after they did, tired and alone.

As she watched them, Kahina sometimes thought how unlike the two brothers seemed at first glance. One had a pale, narrow face; the other's face was round and leathery. One liked to laugh and sing; the other was serious and reflective. And their coats weren't the same colour. Nevertheless, they did resemble each other, and it wasn't hard to mix them up. They had the same way of walking, talking, laughing ... and making love. During the most recent blizzard, when everyone had stayed inside for three days, Tavlo had come twice to lie beside her under the covers, and Akuluk had gone with Nik. This was how they had found out that Nik was expecting another baby. Neither she nor Tavlo had said anything, because they didn't want another child. Kunana wasn't walking yet; he had just cut his first teeth and was beginning to eat seal meat, which his mother was still chewing for him. And all the men said that the times ahead would be difficult.

The days were getting longer. The hunters had time to go very far on the sea ice and stay out for a very long time, but there were few seals. People had lived at the same spot for almost two moons. Even the shaman's invocations were having no effect. They would have to leave soon.

THE PROTOCOL OF SHARING

People everywhere face fluctuations in their food supply. Some are seasonal and predictable, while others strike at random. Throughout most of the world food storage has been the usual form of insurance against hard times. It was certainly employed by the Inuit, who live in one of most precarious and seasonally-extreme environments on earth.

Sealskin buckets were used for hauling and storing water.

Men had long-term partners with whom they shared specific portions of a seal whenever one or the other of them was successful at the hunt, a formal food-sharing system known as pikatigiit.

For the Copper Inuit the predictable lean time was early winter, before they moved out onto the sea ice. Each family tried to bank hundreds of kilos of caribou meat and fish each summer and autumn to last them through this difficult period. They also saved large quantities of seal oil and blubber from the preceding spring, to be used both as food and as fuel.

Techniques of food storage, of course, depend a great deal on climate. During the winter it was easy to let meat freeze on a snow-block platform built outside the house. But at other seasons of the year different techniques were required. Like most Native North Americans, the Copper Inuit depended mainly on drying to preserve meat.

Fish were dried by splitting them down the backbone to the tail, and then turning them inside-out and hanging them. Fishing camps were festooned with cords stretched between piles of rocks, each draped heavily with drying fish. They would then be cached under large piles of boulders — to discourage scavengers — and left until called for.

Caribou or musk-ox meat was also dried, sometimes as large chunks of meat like whole rib cages or complete limbs, and sometimes cut into thinner slices. Because of their comparatively cool, sunny summers the Copper Inuit could do either without seriously spoiling the meat. The fat turns slightly rancid, giving a noticeably bitter taste, and the meat turns nearly black and quite hard. But it is by no means unpalatable, especially when eaten with a little oil or blubber.

Most Inuit, in fact, sometimes deliberately used the storage of meat to change its flavour through a method of controlled fermentation.

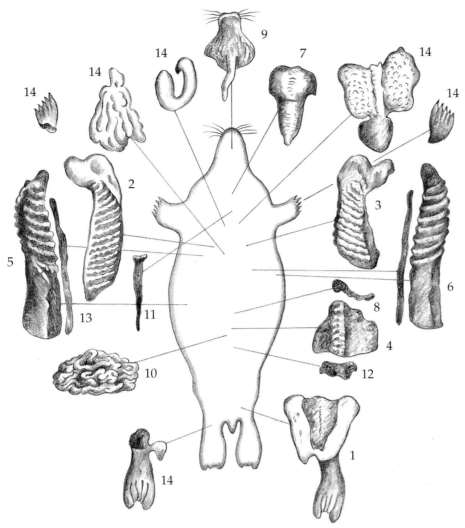

The sharing of a seal, according to one version of the pikatigiit *system (redrawn from Michea,* Esquimaux et Indiens du Grand Nord, *123-24)*

1. the hindquarters with one rear flipper, but without the tail
2. the right back ribs
3. all of the left back ribs except the last five
4. the left bottom four back ribs and the base of the back bone
5. the right side of the belly, with front ribs
6. the left side of the belly, with front ribs
7. the neck and upper spinal column
8. two vertebrae and a left-side rib
9. the head
10. the intestines
11. the sternum (breast bone)
12. the last vertebra on the left side
13. a slice from the left side, and one from the right side
14. the hunter's portion, including the viscera, one rear flipper and the tail, the front flippers, and the blubber from the back, head, and neck.

Meat can be aged safely in oil or blubber for weeks or months at a time. It must be kept out of the sun but open to the air, or food poisoning may result. If done properly it acquires a very strong but delicious flavour. It helped provide variety to a diet that might otherwise become rather monotonous.

Storage was aimed mainly at predictable, seasonal food shortages. The Copper Inuit preferred to deal with more unpredictable, short-term fluctuations through the much more social mechanism of sharing. Sharing promoted the cooperative, egalitarian nature of society, where storage alone would have accentuated the disparity between the relatively well-off and the relatively poor. The Inuit did not practise a type of "primitive communism," but generosity was a social imperative.

Like wife exchange, formal food-sharing partnerships were an important "cement" that held Inuit society together. During the winter seal-hunting season the Copper Inuit and their

Netsilik neighbours practised a system called *pikatigiit*.

Formal systems of food sharing were found among all Inuit. Outside the Central Arctic, most groups restricted formal sharing to larger sea mammals, where hunting was a group effort. Cuts of meat were apportioned out according to a hierarchy that depended on one's position in the boat crew, or whose harpoon first touched the animal. Active participants got by far the largest ration, but as with the Copper Inuit bearded seal hunt even bystanders had the right to something.

There was also informal food sharing, which operated mainly during the summer months. In the winter informal sharing was usually much less generous than *pikatigiit*, and was most common among close relatives and friends. Orphans or others who found themselves outside the more prosperous "sharing circles" could live very hard and miserable lives. But no one was allowed to starve if there was food in the camp.

Cooking was a woman's responsibility, but not a particularly onerous one. In winter all cooking was done over a blubber lamp, soapstone boiling pots were the only cooking vessels, and seal meat essentially the only food.

In winter breakfast was eaten whenever people awoke. A very simple meal, it was usually just leftovers from the night before. Dinner was the main meal, and a good wife had it ready when her husband returned at the end of the day. If it was not quite ready he would often undress and eat in bed, particularly if the day had been a long one.

Winter dinners almost always consisted of lightly boiled seal meat and broth. To prepare the meal the woman hung her soapstone pot over the lamp and filled it with crushed snow. As the snow melted she placed pieces of seal meat into the cold water and brought it slowly to a boil. When the water boiled, the meat was done and was taken out to cool. Seal blood was then added to the water to make a broth, which was ladled into bowls and passed around. It was served with the meat and a little raw blubber.

A DIET OF MEAT—AND OF SOULS

For the Inuit there was no clean or unclean food; they went hungry too often to be squeamish. Any food taboos were individual and usually temporary. Shamans, for instance, sometimes decreed that a sick person refrain from eating certain foods.

This bone or antler Copper Inuit fork was used for serving meat from the cooking pot.

Of far greater importance was an entire system of rules governing how food animals were to be treated. Animal spirits were powerful, and easily offended. It was essential that they be afforded the proper respect, since a mistreated spirit could turn into a bloodthirsty monster. By treating the spirit with respect the good hunter ensured continued hunting access to the animal, which would be reborn to be hunted again. In a way, a careful hunter was always hunting the same animal. As one shaman explained, Inuit life was particularly dangerous because "we live on a diet of souls."

Since they live in salt water, seals and other sea mammals were thought to be perpetually thirsty. Their souls were therefore pleased by being offered a drink of water. Birds on the other hand had a longing for oil. Before being skinned or plucked the bird's head, feet, and wing joints were rubbed with a little oil. Caribou would be gravely offended if their bones were gnawed by dogs near the place where they had been killed.

Wolves and bears had to be treated with the utmost respect, or they could be extremely dangerous. A dead male was offered a tiny bow as a hunting gift. A female would receive a strip of hide that could be used as a needle holder, or even real needles. These animals were like people and needed the same things. No sewing could be done on the day following a killing.

The first time a boy killed a major game animal like a seal or caribou, his mother had to pretend to weep and wrestle with her son over the animal, giving it the impression that she was sorry it had been killed. Anyone who mocked a game animal or delighted in needless pain would find himself cursed by bad luck or struck down by illness.

Failure to observe the proper ritual behaviour with regard to animals would offend not only their spirits but also the spirits of the air, and even the sky itself. Kannakapfaluk, the Mistress of Sea Mammals and the most powerful of all spirits, would also grow angry and humans would starve. Hunting was a very dangerous way to make a living, both physically and spiritually.

This Copper Inuit serving dish is made of wood.

Another crucial ritual observance was the proper separation of the products of land and sea. The Copper Inuit year was divided into a winter half, spent on the sea ice, and a summer half, spent on the land. Should the products of land and sea, of summer and winter, come into contact with one another, the spirits who control people's fates would be gravely displeased.

This ritual separation touched nearly every aspect of Copper Inuit life. Since caribou are a land animal all caribou-skin clothing had to be sewed on land, normally in the autumn or early winter before people moved out onto the sea ice. Conversely, it was forbidden to sew sealskin on land, particularly when people were camped at fishing creeks

Water bucket

Lamp

Board, or hearth

Hole for inserting the tip of the drill shaft

Sinew line with handles, for rotating the shaft

Hole for inserting the tip of the drill shaft

Drill shaft

Mouthpiece or bearing

Greenlandic fire-making equipment. Many Inuit used friction produced by a bow drill or similar implement to make fire. A second technique employed a spark struck by knocking together lumps of iron pyrites.

The Inuit ate everything that was edible. Food restrictions and taboos were almost always circumstantial and temporary.

while the char were running (freshwater fish were considered land creatures). It was essential that land and sea animal meat not be cooked together in the same pot, or placed alongside each other on the snowhouse platform. Caribou meat and freshwater fish were not to be cooked while living on the sea ice, although they could be eaten raw. Nor could they be cooked on land over a driftwood fire, since driftwood comes from the sea.

Ideas behind this taboo were forceful if somewhat vague. Some said that the Mother of Animals, Kannakapfaluk, would be displeased and in her anger would allow people to starve. Others maintained that the animals themselves were offended, or that the spirits of the dead would grow angry and send disease or storms, or that the sea ice would crack and the village be destroyed. Needless to say, most people were extremely scrupulous.

When European missionaries and fur traders began living among the Inuit, they arrogantly refused to follow these various rules. When divine punishment seemed to pass them by, the Inuit belief in their whole spiritual system was undermined. Attitudes toward nature based on respect and reciprocity were too easily jeopardized by a "rationalistic" ethos based on dominance and exploitation.

FEAR OF FAMINE

Hunger could come at any season and for a number of reasons: the caribou changed their migratory route, the char spawned late, a sick or injured hunter could not find food. Food shortages were the most unforgiving during the cold, dark winter.

Murderous famines began when storms blew for days on end and seal hunting became impossible. One by one the lamps would go out as the precious blubber supplies dwindled, and people would huddle in their cold, dark snowhouses as the wind raged outside. Every night the shamans would interrogate the spirits who controlled the weather, and fear would stalk the community.

Any abatement saw all of the men out hunting for days at a stretch, faces badly frostbitten by the wind. Spare clothing would be eaten, and then the dogs. By this point disaster was already approaching. The adult men were usually the last to go without food, for if they were too weak to hunt, what hope was there for anyone? Sometimes the men would vow not to return until they were successful. They might wait for days beside a breathing hole, knowing that they would not be strong enough to go out again should they come back empty-handed.

If things did not improve, people began to die. Children and the old would go first since they were most vulnerable. Sometimes mothers would kill their own children to spare them what was to come. Cannibalism, and its attendant horrors, followed. Unless they were rescued, the whole camp might perish.

It is difficult to assess how common starvation was in the old days. At a guess, among the Copper Inuit there was real hunger about one winter in every three or four, when a handful of old people might go into a decline but otherwise with no outright deaths. Every six or eight winters a few people might actually starve to death, while every generation saw at least one great calamity, where whole camps would be wiped out and 10 percent of the total population of a region died.

Great famines were sometimes predictable. The worst sequence of events involved a rather cool summer, where melting was incomplete and some of the last winter's ice drifted into the bays and froze in place again in the autumn. This ice cover, broken by the tides into large upturned plates, would be very difficult to travel across. Worse, seals could not cut new breathing holes through this old ice, and would avoid the area after freeze-up. If the situation were widespread, the winter would be difficult, with many deaths and much suffering.

The Central Arctic was the most severely affected region, since people depended on only a few animal species. The Kanghiryuarmiut band of the Copper Inuit lived through several serious starvation episodes at the end of the nineteenth century because of the kinds of ice conditions described above. In the middle of the nineteenth century, a Netsilik band known as the Ukjulingmiut ("the people of the bearded seal") disappeared entirely. The Caribou Inuit, who live on the tundra year-round, probably experienced the most serious famines of all. During the first half of the twentieth century, as the caribou herds failed, their population seems to have declined by as much as 50 percent owing to starvation. Even in the Western Arctic, where people were much better off, fear of hunger is a recurrent theme in traditional stories and art.

The survivors of great famines were marked forever in their bodies and souls. Even though they had been reduced to cannabalism, they were never ostracized socially. They had done what was necessary. Most Inuit died of other causes, including old age, but the fear of starvation was ever-present.

It is not surprising that the primary dietary concern of most Inuit was simply getting enough to eat. They are, of course, famous as "eaters of raw meat" — the usual translation of "Eskimo" (from the Algonkian Indian *askimew*). The description is a relatively fair one. The vast majority of the Inuit diet did consist of meat and fish, and it was often undercooked and sometimes even raw. At one time, so carnivorous a diet struck many Europeans as very curious indeed. How could people eat a balanced diet without fruit and vegetables? We now know that fresh meat is actually a good source of vitamins if it is not overcooked. And the Inuit rarely overcooked their meat.

The Inuit themselves were concerned primarily with fat, not vitamins. As they well knew, a person can half-starve even on plenty of lean meat. It does not provide enough calories, especially for people living an active life in a cold climate. For the Inuit the fatter the meat the better. Their favourite delicacies include aged seal oil and marrow fat, while the ne plus ultra of Inuit cuisine was a substance known in English as "Inuit ice cream" (*akutuq*). It could consist either of boiled and whipped caribou fat mixed with bits of meat and berries, or a mixture of caribou stomach contents and seal oil. Whenever possible every meal was eaten with blubber or fat

as a kind of condiment, and lean dry meat was always eaten with seal oil or a thick slab of back fat.

Our own culture, of course, spends a great deal of effort avoiding fat. But we are much more sedentary than traditional Inuit, who with their high metabolic rates seem to have avoided the potentially unhealthy effects of a high cholesterol or animal fat diet. It was too little rather than too much fat that posed their major health hazard.

This wood-and-hide doll evokes the spirit of winter, the time of games and, sometimes, of starvation. People were forced to remain indoors during stormy weather, and prolonged blizzards could easily result in famine. Any food left was reserved for the hunter, for what hope was there if he was too weak to hunt?

Everyone suffered when the seal hunting failed, not only because of hunger but from cold, since lamps depended on blubber for their fuel. In their distress people were sometimes forced to eat their clothing. And fear grew.

IN THE WORLD OF SPIRITS

The shaman (*angatkuk* in Inuinnaqtun) acted as a mediator between the Inuit and the supernatural world. He (or she) could control various spirits; the spirits of animals, of the dead, or "spirits of the air."

Wooden mask, Alaskan Inuit. A shaman was assisted by various spirit helpers, whom he could summon at need.

Shamanism was not only the religion of the Inuit, but a worldwide phenomenon common to perhaps all of the world's hunting cultures, and underlying later religious developments in much of the rest of the world as well. There is evidence of shamanism dating back 18,000 years in the caves of France, while the word "shaman" itself has a Siberian (Chukchi) origin. Everywhere it is encountered — from the Kalahari Desert to Australia, and from Arctic Europe to South America — shamanism embodies certain fundamental beliefs and attitudes. It is the original religion. So widespread is it, and so ancient, that many people have concluded that it must embody certain fundamental truths about the human psyche.

THE SHAMAN

Summoning and conversing with spirit helpers while in a state of trance is the core experience of shamanism, and shamans were experts in attaining and using this psychological state. Trances were induced through rhythmic drumming, chanting, and mental discipline. In a trance, the shaman could talk with the spirits and was sometimes possessed by them. He (or she) could also make long spiritual journeys, to the bottom of the sea or to the moon.

Despite their powers, shamans were not priests. They did not belong to a religious order, nor were they full-time religious specialists. Most probably saw it as an avenue for personal advancement. But it was the key to Inuit psychological survival.

Among the Copper Inuit anyone could claim to be a shaman, although different shamans were awarded varying levels of respect depending on how well they performed. Both men and women were eligible, although female shamans were usually past childbearing age.

It was believed that a real shaman was born, not made. At birth the infant was lifted up and allowed to look at its afterbirth, a ceremony thought to bestow the gift of prophecy. As an adult the future shaman would begin to acquire spirit helpers. The aspirant would go to a lonely place to fast and suffer, and summon the spirits. Sometimes the spirits would come to a person without being called, since, in a way, it was the spirits who controlled the shaman rather than other way around.

Normally the spirits told the new shaman not to eat certain kinds of food, at the risk of losing his power. Most shamans could count on more than one helping spirit. One man, for instance, was assisted by the spirits of a polar bear, a wolf, and a dog.

As proof of his powers, a shaman performed many miraculous acts. He could fly through the air, swallow fire, sink into the ground or water, or kill and then restore life. Some shamans could change themselves into animals.

Stories about the powers and magical abilities of shamans abound. Some Copper Inuit were once frightened by

Dorset-culture wooden mask, with a particularly demonic, terrifying face. To become a shaman one had to attract and "own" one or more potentially very dangerous spirit helpers.

two Netsilik shamans who drove knives through their own stomachs until the points protruded out their backs without any harm. Ilatsiak, one of the most famous of Copper Inuit shamans, went into an empty snowhouse and turned himself into a polar bear. He then frightened away the two Netsilik shamans.

On another occasion a Bathurst Inlet shaman named Pannaktak once told a man to stand up with his back to the wall of the dance house. He then drove his harpoon right through the man's chest. The man had to be held up to keep him from falling. The shaman then made the harpoon return through the chest, leaving the man whole and unhurt.

Many of these "miraculous" events were of course performed through sleight of hand and other tricks. Successful shamans were skilled performers, and were much aided by a sympathetic, credible audience. They were not charlatans, however, even when they knowingly engaged in tricks. They were simply increasing their own prestige through a good show. They, like their audience, believed entirely in their spirit helpers and the powers they could confer. Even for the sceptic, it should be clear that shamanism performed a crucial role. It gave people the illusion that they could control things they could not really control: illness, bad weather, poor hunting, all of the problems of a cold and dangerous world. It inspired hope and kept despair at bay when times were hard, and enriched people's lives with drama and colour. On a deep level shamanism allowed society to be in touch both with itself and with the natural world.

IN THE TIME OF FEAR AND FAMINE

Most of a shaman's more important tasks revolved around fear; fear of the unknown, fear of disaster. Malevolent spirits were an ever-present source of danger, and one that only the shaman could dispel. It sometimes happened that a village or camp was attacked by evil spirits, usually spirits of the dead that had grown wicked with age. They could be killed by the shaman in a seance.

The greatest of all spirits was Kannakapfaluk, who lived with a dwarf named Unga in a snowhouse at the bottom of the sea. If people violated any of her taboos — for instance by cooking caribou meat on the sea ice, or sewing too much during the dark days of winter — Unga gathered all the seals into their undersea snowhouse and people starved. The shaman then held a seance in the dance house, which was of course built on the sea ice. He would lower a long rope through the floor of the house with a noose at the end. Everyone would gather around the rope and sing a well-known incantation:

The woman down there she wants to go away.
Some of the young seagulls I can't lay my hands on.

A second Dorset-culture mask, this time with a happier visage. In many areas it was believed that illness took the form of a small object that the shaman could suck from the patient's body.

Animal souls often numbered among the spirit helpers of a shaman.

This Thule figurine less than 4 cm high was found in the Copper Inuit region. It seems to depict a shaman. Incised lines on the sides and back indicate the position of the bones beneath the skin, a common theme in shamanic art.

That man he can't right matters by himself.
Over where no people dwell,
I go myself to make things right.

Shamans loved riddles and had a dread of naming concrete things. The "young seagulls" here were probably seals, while "that man" would be the shaman himself. When the song was over, the shaman slipped the noose over Kannakapfaluk's wrists and hauled her up from the bottom of the sea until her head was just below the level of the floor. He must not draw her up too high, for she would be furious if the people saw her. The shaman would talk with her, explaining that the people were hungry, and begging her to release the seals. Then he lowered her down again, and she would order Unga to let the seals go.

Long periods of bad weather were sometimes caused by the "weather's opening" coming ajar, causing suffering and starvation. A shaman could close the weather's opening and end the storm. A seance would be called in the dance house. After achieving the proper spiritual state, the shaman ran out into the open air naked from the waist up, except for a headband made of the long breast hair of a caribou. With the help of his spirits, the weather's opening could be plugged with the headband.

FOR PRIVATE HIRE

Not all of a shaman's duties were involved with the welfare of the whole community. He could also be hired privately. When someone became ill, he or she would send a present to the shaman, preferably something valuable like a dog or a sled. The shaman would then hold a seance in the house of the sick person to ascertain the cause of the illness. In most cases, it was determined that evil spirits had attacked the person, possibly because of the breach of some taboo. In one case, a man's sickness was caused by his having treacherously hid a bearded seal that he had killed, without sharing it with the other hunters. In most instances, discovery of the cause and confession of any wrongdoings effected the cure.

In dreams, or by speaking directly with the spirits, a shaman could learn things hidden from other men. Small fetishes were sometimes carved as homes for the spirits, and were asked questions. Shamans were often commissioned to find lost objects, or to discover the truth in some dispute.

THE REVERSE OF THE COIN

Shamans could also use their powers to hurt others, and were commonly believed to do so. This often resulted in trouble, for any suspicious or unexpected death was usually ascribed to shamanic witchcraft. Some shamans promised magical revenge for various personal offenses. One threatened to make a man stumble and fall every few steps. In another tale, a shaman killed two men who had kidnapped his daughter by magically causing their kayaks to capsize, drowning them. Sometimes crude human figures made of bark were used as fetishes and stabbed with knives to cause pain and injury to the person represented. Or a shaman and his spirit helpers could simply steal someone's soul until that person died.

Occasionally a particularly wicked shaman could cause even wider destruction. In one story set in the fairly recent past, a succession of blizzards along the south shore of Dolphin and Union Strait kept the people there on the point of starvation. Finally someone actually starved to death, and a seance was held. The father-in-law of Uloksak, who was himself a well-known shaman in the early twentieth century, was then one of the principal shamans in the area. He held a grudge against the people because they had killed one of his relatives. So with the aid of his spirit helpers, in the middle of the seance he deliberately knocked down one of the pillars erected in ancient times to hold up the sky. The sky fell and many people were killed.

If society allows a shaman to possess supernatural powers, it must expect those powers to be sometimes misused. But murder was murder, and a shaman suspected of killing by witchcraft was likely to end up on the point of someone's knife.

This shaman's costume from northwest Hudson Bay is an exact, locally made duplicate of one worn by the shaman Qingailisaq in the late 19th century. The original was made following a vision. The open hand served to ward off evil spirits. In Siberia, especially, shamans commonly wore a special costume when performing, but this practice was very rare in the Canadian Arctic.

CHAPTER 6

THE PRIZE OF SURVIVAL

The decision was made very quickly. As soon as the baby was born, one of the women who had assisted Nik took it outside and placed it, naked, on the sea ice. Nik had not asked to see it. The infant died without a cry.

The new village site had turned out to have very few seals, and a blizzard had been blowing for days and days. Everyone was hungry and cold and scared, even the shaman, who had gone under the sea three times to implore the Big Woman to free the seals. Each time, he had returned terrified by what he had seen and heard, and now he had shut himself in his snowhouse and wouldn't talk to anyone. One by one, the lamps went out. Every night, the wind carried groans, cries, weeping. No woman would want to bring a child into the world under these circumstances.

The explorer Vihljálmur Stefánsson named the Copper Inuit because of their use of raw, native copper for a variety of tools. Observing blue eyes among some of them, he also advanced the theory that the Copper Inuit were in part a remnant of the lost Norse colony from Greenland. Diamond Jenness refuted this suggestion, noting that blue eyes were found only among the older men, and were the result of chronic snow blindness.

If it had been a boy, Nik's friend, Agara, who had lost her baby earlier in the winter, might have wanted to keep it in spite of the famine and the difficult migration that they would soon have to make to the coast. But Agara would never keep a girl. The spirits were already too angry.

Then one night, the wind fell and a full moon emerged from behind the clouds. The voices hushed, hopeful that the worst had

passed. The next day, the men were able to go out to hunt and when they came back with a few seals, everyone knew the shaman's pleas had finally been answered.

Akuluk brought a seal for Kahina to butcher. Everyone had a share of the meat, even Akuluk's father — Kahina took him the leftovers after the dogs had been well fed. No one had the heart to dance or sing, but at least it was warm in the snowhouse for the first time in a long while.

Even though clear skies had returned, the Kanghiryuarmiut could not relax. Every day, when the sun was at its highest, big puddles formed on the sea ice and soon, there would be wide crevasses. It was time to leave the sea ice. Most people were planning on camping along the coast, where they could fish through the ice and perhaps go inland after a few skinny caribou. Despite the warmer weather, the damp and wet at this time of year was always uncomfortable, and nearly everyone would come down with a mild cold. But at least winter was over, Kahina thought.

The trip to the coast was horrible. Everyone was exhausted and miserable. They had eaten some of the dogs during the famine, and the ones that were left were so thin and feeble they could hardly pull the sleds. During the day the snow was heavy and sticky and pulled at everyone's feet, so it was easier to travel after the sun went down when the snow became firm and crunchy. Nik was so weak and hungry that she had little milk for Kunana; some of the time, Kahina or Agara carried him under their coats. Everyone knew that Tavlo and Akuluk had resolved that it was time for their father to die. Akuluk had packed his father's things on the sled, but no one would help the old man or even look at him. He was having

Although many men died in accidents, women probably suffered more from ill health. A lifetime of winters spent in a sometimes smoky, poorly ventilated house could result in serious, chronic respiratory problems.

An old hunter would try to remain useful for as long as possible.

trouble keeping up; he was always far behind, a tiny shape in the moonlight. No one turned around, but they felt his presence behind them. It made Akuluk so nervous and aggressive that he hit his dogs for no reason.

His father had once been strong, talented, and courageous. He must have been or he wouldn't have survived. He had taught Akuluk and Tavlo everything they knew: how to hunt seals on the sea ice, how to conduct a caribou drive, how to build a weir to trap the schools of char swimming upstream in the spring, and how to make harpoons, kayaks, and sleds. He had known how to do everything.

But now he could do very little. According to Tavlo, he had only killed a single seal all winter — and he had needed help to pull it out of the water. Akuluk was stunned that his father couldn't see what a dead weight he had become to his family. He had gone from being a great hunter to living on charity. This enraged Akuluk. He wanted to strike his father when he accepted meat from others; he should have refused even leftovers. Their mother had been stronger. She had been a good seamstress and, according to the old people, a lover sought by all the men. When she went blind and realized that she was a burden, she let herself die.

But this crazy old man was clinging to life. The young people laughed at him and no one listened to him any more. He was pitiable. In Akuluk, grief and embarrassment had transformed the pity into anger. His father understood and didn't go near him any more.

When they reached the coast, they stopped. It was very late at night. Akuluk and Tavlo found a patch of good snow and built a little shelter against a cliff. They laid a small piece of seal meat in it, then all the people waited quietly for the old man. When he arrived, Akuluk helped him lie down in the shelter and placed his harpoon near him, and then everyone immediately left without a word or a backward glance.

For a long time, they saw behind them in the moonlight the tracks of the sleds, the dogs, and the people, and the small snowhouse in which the old man was lying. And then everything was lost in the bright light of dawn.

The next day, Akuluk began to talk about his father, about what a great and courageous hunter he had been. And about how, when he felt that he was old and useless, he had asked that they build him a snowhouse in which he could die. He had been a great man.

THE HARDSHIPS OF LIFE

Life for the Inuit has always been dangerous. They share their world with fierce animals, terrible storms, and murderous cold. The sea ice is treacherous and deceptive, and even in summer the water so cold it can kill in a few minutes. There are a thousand ways to die. And if, exceptionally, one died of old age, having avoided a thousand ills, a thousand perils, old age was still not very old. In traditional times, few could have lived much beyond 60 or 65. Old age was rare.

Like this Alaskan Inuit shaft wrench, the objects of daily life were sometimes beautifully decorated.

Life expectancy in the past is difficult to estimate. Analysis of a population of 150 early Inuit skeletons from Southampton Island, north of Hudson Bay, suggests that the oldest adult male died at the age of about 45, the oldest female at 55. These results seem grim indeed, but may not be altogether representative. Throughout the Central Arctic in the early twentieth century there were certainly individuals who must have been in their 50s or 60s, although precise age is usually impossible to determine, since Inuit did not keep track of their ages.

For the few who did live long enough, old age could be a misery. Crippled by rheumatism or arthritis, half-blind and half-toothless, the elderly quickly became a burden, and sometimes an unsupportable one. When times were hard, when camps had to be moved and there was not enough food to go around, the difficult decision would be made to do away with the old, to abandon a mother or father. A small snowhouse was built as both shelter and tomb, a little food was left, and the group moved on. There were no goodbyes, no backward glances. Only later, when life was more secure, would people stop to remember.

Finding that life was no longer worth living, the elderly sometimes killed themselves. For a people as fiercely independent as the Inuit, old age could be particularly bitter. Charity, even the charity of one's own children, could be hard to suffer, and as non-producers the elderly were afforded comparatively little respect. An old hunter remembering the days of his youth, or an old woman her many lovers, would sometimes become depressed and decide to end it all. Hanging was a usual means of suicide, sometimes assisted by a favoured adult child. Perhaps because old age was so rarely attained in the

An old woman sits on the sleeping platform, tending her own lamp.

Central Arctic, suicide by the elderly was comparatively rare among the Copper and Netsilik Inuit. It was much more common in many other areas of the Arctic.

It was not only older people who fell victim to the hardships of life. A very important factor affecting the population structure was the practice of female infanticide. The Copper Inuit and many of their neighbours, including the Netsilik, killed a significant percentage of baby girls at birth, simply because they could not afford to keep them. Girls, it was felt, contributed little to the family's well-being, since by the time they were old enough to be useful they were married. Boys, on the other hand, would start bringing home food by the time they were ten or twelve, and could be relied on more readily than a son-in-law for support and help in old age.

Normal methods of killing included exposure, quick and comparatively painless in cold weather, and suffocation. Infanticide was particularly common for children born during the summer, since parents could carry only one child at a time on their long summer wanderings. Census figures from the early twentieth century suggest that as many as one in two female babies was killed at birth.

Female infanticide affected the population structure in several ways. Obviously by markedly lowering the number of girls who lived through infancy it decreased the number of women able to bear children, and hence acted as a brake on population in the next generation. A little more subtly it affected male mortality as well. Since there were not enough women of marriageable age to go around, access to women was a major point of contention between men and the central issue in many a murder. Women were almost never murdered; men not uncommonly were. Men also suffered a much higher death rate from accidents: drowning, freezing, falling through the ice, complications from injuries, hunting mishaps, and so on. Boys might outnumber girls by a ratio of nearly two to one, but about as many women as men lived to see old age.

The prevalence of infanticide in the Central Arctic was not due to cultural depravity or cruelty but to the inexorable demands of a harsh environment. And it worked. It helped to keep population growth in check in an area with a very limited carrying capacity. And it helped keep the sexual ratio at an optimum balance, one which favoured male food producers without too much endangering reproductive success in the next generation.

All Inuit engaged in some infanticide, but only in the Central Arctic was it a major factor in population dynamics. Elsewhere it was largely limited to handicapped or deformed babies, or to orphans too young to survive without their mother's milk. In other areas people could usually afford to raise all of their children.

ILLNESS AND DEATH

Knowledge of rates and types of disease among traditional Inuit is very limited. In the case of the Copper Inuit, for instance, there is almost no detailed information before the late 1920s, by which time people were already beginning to suffer from a number of imported infectious diseases, especially tuberculosis. It is ironic that the very people supplying the earliest medical records — doctors, missionaries, and police — were among the same people whose very presence was destroying traditional health patterns.

With no resistance to "outside" infectious diseases, the Inuit everywhere suffered shocking population losses in the first generations after contact. Large quantities of scattered human bone around the Bathurst Inlet area, for instance, bear witness to a major epidemic among eastern Copper Inuit, which oral tradition dates to sometime in the early nineteenth century. In parts of the Western Arctic, there were population declines of as much as ninety percent during the nineteenth century as the result of imported diseases. As well as tuberculosis, measles, influenza, and possibly smallpox have been major killers in the Arctic.

It is difficult to get a clear picture of Inuit health before the contact epidemics. On an impressionistic level, an early visitor to the Copper Inuit described them as a very healthy people, almost disease-free aside from the occasional spring cold. The principal causes of death were said to be old age, murder, infanticide, starvation, and especially accidents, "the various perils that are inseparable from life in the Arctic." Similar statements are echoed by other early Arctic travellers.

This is a widely held point of view, and one containing a great deal of truth. At the same time, however, it is somewhat too simple. If they suffered little from infectious diseases, it is becoming increasingly clear that traditional Inuit still had a number of serious health problems, mostly of an environmental nature.

The relevant information is archaeological in origin. Frozen, sometimes partially mummified human bodies dating to well before the period of European contact have been found near Point Barrow, Alaska, and on the western coast of Greenland. All of the adults are women, and present a similar picture of less-than-ideal health. Autopsies have revealed evidence of pneumonia, kidney problems (including stones), trichinosis, and repeated periodic malnutrition, manifested in growth-arrest lines on the long bones (Harris lines). There was also abundant evidence of degenerative diseases of the bones and teeth (for example, osteoarthritis, osteoporosis, periodontitis), and of chronic anthracosis ("black lung"), caused by a lifetime of exposure to lamp soot in a poorly ventilated environment. One woman suffered from a large abdominal cyst, another from a fatal facial cancer, and a third from a fractured clavicle that had been broken at least a year before death, but which never healed because of constant stress on the arm.

Most Inuit probably suffered from similar ailments. Indeed, Alaskan and Greenlandic Inuit lived lives which were, on average, a little easier than those of the Copper Inuit and their Central Arctic neighbours.

Traditional remedies were mostly supernatural, for the causes of disease were generally felt to lie within the spiritual realm. Witchcraft, the influence of evil spirits, or the breaking of some taboo were the usual diagnoses. Cures thus revolved around confession, or various forms of shamanic aid. A shaman, for instance, might "find" and remove a small foreign object from the patient's body, believed to have been placed there by magical means to cause sickness. Or she could determine that an illness was caused by a malicious spirit, which could then be placated. Although not practically helpful (by our way of thinking), traditional medical practices such as these

Wooden sculpture of a man, Alaskan Inuit. The greatest danger menacing the Inuit came from the qablunaq, who brought into the Arctic a multitude of evil spirits: infectious diseases, deadly viruses and bacteria against which the Inuit had no remedies or defenses.

must have helped improve the patient's psychological well-being.

Nor were all remedies purely spiritual. Many maladies, such as broken bones, were obviously physical in origin, and had physical cures. Even infectious diseases were not always strictly a spiritual matter, as a tragic collision between Inuit and English medical practices that occurred in 1822 illustrates.

In that year the explorer William Parry was wintering near the Melville Peninsula northwest of Hudson Bay. An epidemic broke out in the neighbouring Inuit camps, causing widespread illness and several deaths. In the best humanitarian tradition, Parry quickly established a hospital to bring the benefits of English medical science to bear on the problem. The Inuit avoidance of the sick, and their refusal to drink from the same cup or use the same eating implements as those who were ill aroused strong disapproval among the English, who interpreted such behaviour as simple pagan superstition. In their hospital they enforced a close intimacy, resolving "if possible to cure the Esquimaux even in spite of themselves." Eventually they concluded that the symptoms were caused by overeating meat! Needless to say they did not make a significant dent in the death rate.

The Inuit were not afraid of death, for it was a commonplace despite all religious or practical attempts to control it. They were afraid of the dead, however. It was imperative that they be well treated, otherwise the spirit of the dead person would certainly become evil and attempt to revenge itself upon the living. The unappeased dead hated the living and were the usual cause of winter storms and starvation.

Among the Copper Inuit, a new corpse was bound with thongs to keep it harmless, and laid "in state" in the house or tent in which the person had lived for three days, if a man, or four if a woman. During that time death taboos were observed by the household. No sewing could be done, nor could hair be combed, yet there was no prohibition against hunting; a seal or caribou could be brought into the death house, butchered, and eaten, although the skin could not be used for clothing. Knives were laid on the sleeping platform between the corpse and the rest of the household as they slept at night, possibly to protect the living from the spirit of the dead person. After lying in state, the corpse was removed through a hole cut in the back wall so that watching spirits might not see it. The house or tent would then be abandoned, along with the deceased's clothing and sleeping robes.

In a rocky, frozen land, the dead could not be buried. Instead, the corpse was laid out on the ground within a circle of small stones, called an *ilovgak*. No attempt was made to build a rocky cairn over the body, or to cover it with piled driftwood, as was done in other areas of the Arctic. When laid in the *ilovgak*, the thongs binding the corpse were cut, allowing the spirit to go free. Some or all of the dead person's tools were placed with the body for use in the spirit world. They were broken first, since the dead use dead tools. Sometimes miniature copies were substituted for the more valuable items.

Those who handled the corpse were subject to a few temporary taboos. After leaving the grave, they had to drink water upon arriving home, so that the dead person might not thirst. And they had to share a piece of blubber from the first animal killed after the funeral with each of their fellow villagers, who in turned placed it in the lamp, where it was burned.

The dead were usually remembered with sadness. The Copper Inuit had no taboos against speaking their names, as did some other Inuit groups. Graves were sometimes visited, unless the person died by violence, in which case the grave site might be haunted by a malicious spirit.

This Alaskan Inuit doll wears labrets.

AN UNSEEN WORLD

Traditional Inuit religious beliefs had no place for a well-ordered pantheon of deities, or even any real gods as other cultures might understand them. Instead, the world of the supernatural was populated by powerful, often malicious spirits. Religious practice was above all concerned with warding off malignant forces in this world, rather than achieving salvation in the next. It was concerned with power and harmony, not morality and ethics.

Without "revealed" dogma or an ordained priesthood, people believed what they wanted, or feared, for in the words of one shaman, "We do not believe; we fear."

The Copper Inuit divided the universe into a number of planes. One was the earth, *nuna*; the flat, unbroken expanse of land stretching on forever, in winter unified with the sea, *tariuq*, by its covering of snow. At the earth's four corners were the pillars that held up the sky.

The sky, *hilak*, was much like the earth: another flat plain, abounding with caribou and other animals. Semi-spiritual beings — the sun, moon, and stars — wandered across this upper expanse.

The weather was considered a being or mighty power living in the sky. Storms issued from holes caused by the malignant spirits of the dead. The stars were people or animals (mostly bears, dogs, and caribou) who for some reason ascended into the sky. The three bright stars of Orion's Belt, for instance, were three lost seal hunters who never returned home. If a rainbow appeared, it was offered a piece of skin to win its favour, for it was believed to be a manifestation of the spirits that bring good weather. Lightning was due to a being named Asiranna shooting his arrows, while the northern lights were thought to be a manifestation of the spirits that bring good weather.

People possessed a number of souls. The personal soul, *nappan*, ceased to exist at death, but the shade or spirit, *tarrak*, continued on, lingering in the place where the body was laid. It could become very dangerous, particularly if the death taboos were not observed. Otherwise its fate was unknown. It was occasionally suggested that the dead might go to the moon, or that they were still alive in some other place. But the majority of Copper Inuit expressed no opinion at all about the conditions or location of the afterworld.

Most other Inuit had more formulated concepts of an afterlife. Many believed in a land in the sky or a kind of underworld filled with animals and other good things. The Netsilik, for instance, thought that the dead might go to one of three places. Lazy hunters, taboo breakers, and untattooed women were stranded in a world of misery and boredom just beneath the surface of the earth, where the only available food was butterflies. There were also two paradises, where game was plentiful: one in the sky, the other deeply buried under the tundra. These were reserved for the best hunters, those who died in accidents, or women who had died in childbirth.

Many Inuit also believed that the souls of the dead were somehow reincarnated in descendants who were named after them. The Copper Inuit had heard of this concept, but had no idea if it was true.

The earth was populated by dangerous spirits and semi-human creatures. Among the latter were whites, *qablunaq*, who in the Central Arctic as late as the early twentieth century were still an almost legendary people, thought to look quite strange indeed (chinless, according to one account). There were also *tornrin*, a race of giants who had been forced to live underground by the shamans. Far away lived a race of Amazons. Elsewhere were people with four eyes, or others with their mouths in their chests. No traveller's tale was too wild to be believed.

There existed three great categories of spirits, all of them potentially dangerous and all of them use-

The Dorset have no heirs, no one we can ask about the meaning of art works like this tiny ivory mask from the Iglulik area. What is apparent, though, is a high degree of technical ability and artistic refinement.

ful as a shaman's spirit helpers: the spirits of the air, the spirits of the dead, and the spirits of animals. Most Inuit religion focused on maintaining a safe and profitable relationship with these beings.

The spirits of the air (*hilap inue*) were a numerous and variable category, living in the sky and in the great open places far from the abodes of men. Although some were monsters, others looked more human, including the little people or dwarfs (*inyuorligat*), who were so short that their bows trailed on the ground behind them as they walked. Then there was

The spirits of the dead and of animals who had not been treated with proper respect could also be dangerous. Long ago, animals lived just like people, and wolves and bears were still sometimes met in human form. Kannakapfaluk, their guardian, was the greatest of all spirits, and at best an ambivalent friend of humans. The breaking of death taboos or any of the rules meant to placate the spirits of animals could quickly result in disaster.

An old Netsilik leader named Qaqortingneq once listed what he thought were his spiritual duties. They can stand for all of the Central Inuit.

Ivory carving of a seal-woman, Alaskan Inuit. In many traditional societies the line between humanity and the natural world was easily crossed.

She seems to wear bracelets around her wrists.

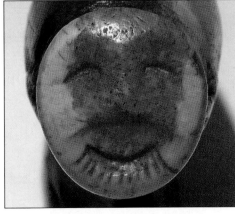

The tattoo lines on the chin leave little doubt as to the sex of our metamorphosed seal-woman.

nighilik ("the one with the hook"), who attacked and knocked down snowhouses. He was much feared, but could be driven away if everyone in the house yelled as loudly as possible.

The *tapluigtut* or "chinless ones" also tried to kill people. Hilaq was a monster in the form of a black bear with huge teeth. It could be seen only by shamans.

I must never offend Nuliajuk [another name for Kannakapfaluk].

I must never offend the souls of animals or a tornraq so that it will strike me with sickness.

When hunting and wandering inland I must as often as I can make offerings to the animals that I hunt, or to the dead who can help me, or to lifeless things, especially stones and rocks, that are to have offerings for some reason or other.

I must make my own soul as strong as I can, and for the rest seek strength and support in all the power that lies in the name.

I must observe my forefathers' rules of life in hunting customs and taboo, which are nearly all directed against the souls of dead people or dead animals.

I must gain special abilities or qualities through amulets.

I must try to get hold of magic words or magic songs that either give hunting luck or are protective.

If I cannot manage in spite of all these precautions, and suffer want or sickness, I must seek help from the shamans, whose mission it is to be the protectors of mankind against all the hidden forces and dangers of life.

THE SUMMER TUNDRA

It is thought that at the moment when it rises above the sea for the first time after the winter solstice, the sun lets out a very soft sigh, which can be heard clearly if one is alone on the sea ice.

In spring, the light spills out in cataracts and whirlpools; it cascades from the clouds and eddies through the snow fields, exploding in the fractured mirror of millions of puddles that dot the sea ice and the rivers and lakes that stretch across the country in uninterrupted chains. As imposing and powerful as the frigid blanket of Arctic night, the brilliance of summer sweeps the North, spreading colour, odour, and song. The sound of running water is everywhere.

By May, it is light twenty-four hours a day and the temperature regularly rises above the freezing point. The snow begins to melt, and the first cracks and leads begin to appear in the sea ice. By the end of June, most of the snow is gone, lingering only on the north side of slopes, or in creek valleys where the sun's rays cannot penetrate. The sea ice has begun to loosen its grip on the shore, and wide shore leads open up. Most of the rivers are running by late June, although some of the larger freshwater lakes remain frozen year-round. Under the combined action of sun, tide, and warm winds the ocean begins to break up during July, although it is nearly the end of the month before boat travel is very practical.

With the spring come the birds. Waterfowl return with the open water in late May: tundra swans, geese, and ducks in immense numbers, for the Arctic is one of the most important nesting areas in the world. Newborn bear cubs and their mothers emerge from snow dens, while the caribou have already left their winter homes in the northern forests and are making their way north to their calving grounds. The wolves follow, ready to pick off the weak or newly born.

THE BLOSSOMING OF SUMMER

The threshold between spring and summer is generally crossed in early July, when two events occur, usually on the same day: the willow leaves appear, and so do the mosquitoes. For the next month or so the latter will dominate the landscape to a degree difficult to imagine if one has not actually experienced it. The Arctic in summer can be sublimely beautiful, but its beauty must always be appreciated through the constant, inescapable hum of its insect life.

The average summer temperature in the Central Arctic is below 10° C, and there are days when the temperature hovers around freezing under a drizzling rain. Frost and snow

Saxifraga oppositifolia
The purple saxifrage is one of over a dozen species of the saxifrage genus that grow in the Arctic, mostly on rock or gravelly soil.

Pedicularis capitata
The louseworts take their name from a old European belief that they favoured the multiplication of lice among herd animals; the Latin pedicularis *preserves the same notion. The dwarf lousewort is found mainly in heathy tundra.*

Papaver radicatum
Arctic poppy is widespread across much of the Arctic. Unlike some of its southern cousins it lacks any narcotic qualities.

can occur at any time, and fogs are common near the coast. But on a nice day — and there are many — the temperature can soar to 15° or 20° C under a cloudless blue sky. A beautiful summer day in the Arctic has no parallel.

Rainy, drizzly days are not uncommon, although it almost never rains hard and precipitation in absolute terms is very low. But even though there is little rainfall, the summer tundra is always wet, the mosses and lichens spongy with water. The permafrost retards drainage; meltwater and rainwater can never evaporate fast enough and lie imponded on the surface. Tundra soil is thin and impoverished. Even at the height of summer, only the top few centimetres thaw. Beneath, the permafrost endures forever, as hard and immobile as cement.

THE TIME OF FLOWERS

Except in areas of exposed bedrock, in Low Arctic latitudes the summer tundra is green with vegetation. There are no trees of course, but in protected locations the normally ground-hugging Arctic willow can grow in dense thickets a metre-and-a-half high. Elsewhere the land is lush with grasses such as foxtail and hair grass and fragrant with Labrador tea.

July is the month of flowers. The white-flowered Arctic aven is one of the prettiest, a pioneer species blooming among the rocks in the most barren and wind-swept areas. Another is the Arctic pyrola or wintergreen, with its creamy white or pinkish blossoms, common on sheltered, sunny slopes. The alpine azalea, another white or pinkish flower, is characteristic of dry rocky areas across the Arctic, as is the Lapland rosebay, with its deep purple, very aromatic blooms. Various species of saxifrage all

bloom in miniature profusion, adding a white and yellow note to the summer tundra.

In August the flowers are replaced by the bright splash of berries. Small, sour blueberries are found in a few more southerly tundra areas. More widespread are crowberries, with purplish-black, very shiny fruit full of large, hard seeds, and cloudberries, with a fruit looking something like an orange, waxy raspberry.

Climate and vegetation do not vary a great deal across the Arctic, but the landscapes show an amazing diversity. Most of the eastern Canadian Arctic is very mountainous, and spectacularly beautiful. Farther west, around Coronation Gulf, the landscapes become more rolling, almost like a northern extension of the Canadian prairies. The Mackenzie is by far the largest Arctic river, huge and slow like the Mississippi, brown with sediment. West of it, the Richardson Mountains in the Yukon and the Brooks Range in Alaska form the northern edge of the Rockies, crowding the coast and forming a magnificent backdrop almost close enough to touch.

Cassiope tetragona and *Pedicularis lanata. Arctic heather, a very common plant in many areas, burns with a hot, resinous flame and was an important source of summer fuel. Woolly lousewort grows well in wetter environments.*

Many tundra landscapes support a rich summer carpet of grasses and mosses, flecked with tiny, bright flowers.

THE HERDS OF SUMMER

For the Inuit, by far the most important game animal on the Arctic tundra was the caribou, *tuktu*. It provided meat, sinew, and above all the hides necessary for warm winter clothing.

South of the High Arctic islands, most Arctic caribou live in large herds that migrate annually between winter ranges in the northern forests and summer ranges on the tundra.

In northern Quebec, on Baffin Island, on the immense tundras of the Canadian Arctic mainland, and in Arctic Alaska, caribou live in large herds numbering tens or hundreds of thousands of animals. They tend to be medium-sized for members of the species *Rangifer tarandus*, with an average male weight of 110 kilograms, smaller than their woodland cousins, but larger than the High Arctic Peary caribou.

Although they represent several distinct subspecies, these tundra caribou all share a migratory way of life. Each year, most animals winter in the northern part of the boreal forest, from Labrador to central Alaska, where trees keep the snow soft enough for foraging through. In the spring they migrate north onto the Arctic tundra, each herd making for its own particular calving grounds, where the females give birth in June.

Each herd is named for its calving grounds. There are four herds on the Central Arctic tundra between Hudson Bay and the Mackenzie River. The Copper Inuit hunt two of them: the Bathurst herd, which calves around the eastern side of Bathurst Inlet, and the Bluenose herd, which calves around Bluenose Lake in the west. In the past, both had ranges which extended north onto Victoria Island. Farther east, the Netsilik are visited by members of the Beverly herd, while most Caribou Inuit hunted the Kaminuriak herd.

In late June the herds disperse across the tundra, feeding widely. In turn, the caribou are preyed upon by wolves. Fortunately, calves are very precocious, and can outrun a wolf within a few days of birth. Aside from very young calves, wolves prey mostly on the old and sick, thus keeping the herd healthy.

In July come the insect hordes, troublesome for humans but far worse for caribou, who are tormented not only by mosquitoes but also by warble and nostril flies. Thin and harrassed, caribou in July are still poor eating, especially the nursing females, and their hides are nearly worthless.

By August the insects begin to subside and caribou can start to put on weight again. At this season they often bunch up into large, dense herds which can be very productively ambushed at watercrossings or similar strategic locations. By September

the bulls are in prime condition, as are any non-breeding cows. Cows with calves, on the other hard, are still fairly thin. The demands of pregnancy and particularly of lactation mean that females remain in poor shape until winter. Inuit hunters were well aware of this and selectively targeted bulls during the main September hunt.

In October the caribou begin to migrate south toward the tree line. In the days when caribou still summered on Victoria Island, they would gather along the south coast waiting for the ocean to freeze, making the crossing usually in November. In November too comes the rut or breeding season. By the end of this exhausting ordeal winter is at hand, and the herds disappear into the forest for another season. A few linger throughout the winter in protected valleys or windswept areas where the browse is adequate, but the Inuit rarely saw them since they chose themselves to winter far out on the sea ice.

Barrenground caribou (Rangifer tarandus groenlandicus) *live on the tundra west of Hudson Bay, on Baffin Island, and in Greenland. The caribou of Arctic Quebec belong to a different subspecies* (R.t. caribou), *but behave in many ways like their barrenground cousins.*

A RAMPART OF HORNS

The musk-ox, *umingmak*, is not migratory, but a year-round inhabitant of the Arctic tundra. A shaggy creature with great drooping horns, it bears a superficial resemblance to the bison.

It is more closely related, however, to sheep and goats. It is also smaller than might be expected from photographs. Adult bulls stand no more than about 135 centimetres at the shoulder and weigh about 340 kilos. Much of their apparent bulk is made up of hair. Musk-ox have two coats of hair, a soft inner coat as fine as cashmere, called *qiviut*, and an outer layer of long, coarse guard hairs.

They are a mildly gregarious animal, living in small herds ranging from three to a hundred animals, with an average of about fifteen. For much of the year these herds often include only the cows, calves, and younger bulls. The older bulls generally wander about alone or in small groups, but join the cow herds in July, forming harems. They drive off other intruding bulls and often engage in serious head-butting contests. The rut occurs in August, and the calves are born the following April or May.

Although they look fierce, musk-ox are generally mild-mannered, except during the rut. They will, however, sometimes charge if provoked. They have excellent eyesight and acute hearing, and although usually slow and stolid are capable of bursts of real speed. They are mobile feeders.

Two hundred years ago musk-ox were found nearly everywhere across the top of North America, from eastern Greenland to Alaska. Largely because of over-

The Inuit word for musk-ox, umingmak, *means "bearded one." This species became extinct in the Old World several thousand years ago.*

hunting they were in steep decline by the early twentieth century, but with government protection have since recovered. The present Canadian population numbers an estimated 85,000 animals, probably about the same as it did in the eighteenth century. These animals live almost everywhere in the Copper Inuit region.

The heavy winter coat of the musk-ox is proof against even the coldest winter weather. They are still vulnerable to poor weather conditions, however, particularly freezing rain or unusually deep snow cover. Because of their well-known habit of forming a defensive ring when attacked, they are also easily hunted by people armed with rifles or even bows.

SUMMER WANDERERS

Barrenground grizzly bears live everywhere on the mainland tundra west of Hudson Bay. Winter hibernators, they are often encountered during the summer. They tend to be a little smaller than their Rocky Mountain cousins, averaging perhaps 200 or 250 kilos for males. This is certainly large enough; grizzlies are an unpredictable and potentially dangerous animal, often

attracted to camps by the smell of food. The Inuit feared them far more than polar bears because of their readiness to fight when cornered; in at least one traditional Inuit story the bear is quoted as saying, "I am not afraid of men."

Smaller carnivores are widespread in the Arctic, including wolves, two species of foxes — Arctic and red — and wolverines. Of the smaller animals, ground squirrels are one of the most characteristic and abundant. They inhabit small colonies on the higher, better drained slopes where permafrost is not too much of a hindrance to their burrowing activities.

The summer tundra also abounds with nesting waterfowl. Important species include tundra swans, many species of geese, among them the white-fronted goose, snow goose, and Canada goose, as well as various ducks, including northern pintail, eider, king eider, and old squaw. All were avidly pursued by the Inuit, especially during the summer moult. So too were loons, of which several species summer in the area. Waterfowl are all migratory species, arriving with the first open water in early June, and staying until freeze-up begins in September.

When attacked, musk-ox sometimes form a defensive ring, presenting predators with a rampart of horns. Wolves try to break the circle by panicking the animals into fleeing, thus exposing calves and other vulnerable individuals to attack.

CHAPTER 7

DAYS WITHOUT END

Since childhood, Akuluk and Tavlo had been contradicting each other. They were never angry when they disagreed — it was more like a game. Akuluk would say that he liked summer more than any other season because the weather was warm and the sky was always changing. The spirits were in a good mood, and he was free to do all sorts of different things; Tavlo would shout back that he liked the clear, clean cold of winter, and life on the sea ice when all the people were together and there were dances, songs, and games in the dance house.

Diamond Jenness spent the summer of 1915 with his Copper Inuit hosts hunting and fishing on southwestern Victoria Island. Here his adopted father and mother, Ipakhuak and Higilak, load up for a camp move.

But after this winter, one of the hardest and saddest that they had known in some time, the brothers didn't argue, not even in fun. Summer seemed to everyone to be a deliverance.

It would take a long time to get over the famine. Of course, the people and dogs had rapidly regained their strength, but they had no blubber in reserve. Worst of all, the caches in which they usually placed blubber reserves for the following autumn were empty. What would the women use for light when they were sewing the winter clothing? How would they heat the tents and snowhouses while they were waiting for the ice to form and the seal hunt to begin?

But right now, it didn't matter. The wind was warm and full of the rich odours of earth and sea. The sky was light and full of birds. There was colour and movement everywhere — on the beaches, in the lakes and rivers, very far away in the sea, very high in the sky. The long night had finally lifted, and no one was cold or hungry or scared any more.

One day, Akuluk and Kahina lay down together on the thick, dry moss on the slope of a sun-drenched glen. The winds swept away the mosquitoes and brought all the scents and songs of summer. Life felt soft and exciting ... It was the voice of Kannakapfaluk, the Mother of All Animals, that awoke them. Hidden under the sea, Kannakapfaluk was singing very softly. In that instant, Kahina believed, a spirit entered her with the Good Woman's song and a child began to grow.

She sometimes remembered the people of Noahognir and wondered, with an anguished heart, how they had survived the winter. But in the soft warmth of the long days, her anxieties quickly vanished. Like Akuluk, she preferred summer. There was much more to be done, but it was also more varied. Alone or with Nik or Akuluk, she strolled through fields of lichen or around marshes covered with white tufts of cottongrass, and dreamed that the good weather

By May the warming sun made the heavy spring tent a practical alternative to the dripping roof of a snowhouse.

Copper Inuit families could not afford to feed a team of more than two or three dogs. With their sled piled high for a winter village move, husband and wife must help pull.

would last forever and they would never want for anything again. She collected heather for the fire, and berries to add variety to their diet. She set snares to catch ground squirrels and was secretly proud of her success rate. Once, she managed to snare an ermine. She took special pains over preparing the skin and cut out a handsome pendant that she would attach to her winter coat.

Sometimes, she went with Nik to gather eggs. Flocks of ducks, geese, and swans would rise from the tundra, wheeling above them with piercing cries. Nik, quick and accurate with a stone, would bring down as many as she could while Kahina raided the nests.

Of course, she missed her friends sometimes — not just the Noahognirmiut, but also Agara and the others who had come

every day through the winter to chat. After they had cached their winter gear, the Kanghiryuarmiut had spread out in small groups across the tundra. Kahina didn't know where they might be. Some groups had probably gone far into the interior, while others would be meandering along the coast without any definite destination.

Although Akuluk would have liked to stay by the shore, Tavlo insisted that they retrace the exact path their father used to take and find the same river fords, fishing spots, and camps that they had always known. Sometimes, they lost their way and had to search long and hard in the rolling, stone-strewn hills and dales for the signs that their father had found so easily, never hesitating. But finally, in no small part thanks to the dogs, they found the wide river they were looking for and located the old weirs, which had been breached by floodwaters and broken by ice. They had to go into the swift, icy water up to the waist, their legs bare, to find and replace the stones one by one. Everything seemed easier in the summer, so the work was like a game, everyone laughing and forgetting the time and their fatigue.

When the schools of char arrived, they filled the basins that the weirs had made on the river. With long tridents, Akuluk, Tavlo, and Nik picked them out of the water one by one, nice white-and-pink fish. They would be set out on racks to dry in the warm sun and later stored in their caches. Kahina was not allowed to help them. Tavlo said that she would scare the fish away or keep them from entering the basins, while it was Akuluk's opinion that it was too dangerous for the child she was carrying; she might miscarry, or her son would be awkward all his life and never become a good hunter. It came to the same thing, Kahina thought: either way, she couldn't go and take part in the work and the games. Making a baby was a lonely matter.

115

TOWARD THE LAND OF SUMMER

With the warming days of early May, winter life slowly drew to a close. Snowhouse roofs began to leak and sag in the warm afternoon sun, and people moved into their heavy spring tents. At first they were usually pitched inside a low wall of snowblocks, and equipped with an entrance tunnel for warmth.

This beautifully carved ivory whip handle was used by Inuit who could afford to run a large team.

As a kind of half-tent, half-snowhouse, this dwelling was well suited to the season. With the longer days the men concentrated their activities on seal hunting, trying to lay up a good store of blubber for the coming autumn.

The end of the sealing season usually came early in the second half of May, when wide shore leads and cracks in the ice meant that seals would no longer keep to their breathing holes. Copper Inuit were rarely interested in stalking basking seals on the spring ice. They hungered for a change of scenery, and of diet. It was time to go. Sleds were packed, dogs were harnessed, and people began to move off the ice.

A number of well-known trails led from the coast into the interior, and people would make for the one leading to the area where they planned to spend the summer. In most cases this meant that the large winter villages were dissolved almost overnight into two or three parties

headed for different summering grounds. Travel was comparatively slow and easy, covering perhaps 15 or 20 kilometres a day. Camp would be pitched each night. If the weather was warm they might sleep by day and travel at night, when freezing temperatures would help firm up the snow.

The spring tent of a prosperous family was large and heavy, weighing about 30 kilos and taking up a good deal of space on the sled. When pitched it often had a larger floor area than the snowhouse, standing a little over two metres high, and measuring about

Dog sledding was a slow and often frustrating task. Owners often had to separate fighting dogs and untangle traces foul with excrement.

In the brilliant light of spring, people and dogs haul this family's few possession to a fishing lake near the coast. Only the very youngest have the luxury of riding.

behind the sled, the heavy blubber lamp, or the spring tent, all of which were still important conveniences. But some winter clothing could be left behind, along with hunting gear and the sealskins full of oil and blubber that had been saved for the coming autumn.

Often the spring migration party would break up again on reaching the coast. Or people might stay together for days or weeks because of individual needs and local conditions. The transition from large winter villages into the tiny bands of summer proceeded piecemeal, depending on a host of separate decisions.

In late May caribou were abundant, both on the mainland and crossing the ice to calving grounds on Victoria Island. Most people paid little attention to them, for they were generally thin and in poor condition at this time of year. A family or two might go off for a few days or weeks to hunt them, but more for a change in diet than anything else.

In spring and early summer fish not caribou were the main source of food. Some families lingered near the sea coast to jig through the ice for tomcod. Others travelled into the interior to well-known fishing lakes to jig for trout or char, or to spear them from the edge of the now rapidly melting ice. As the season progressed, groups tended to get smaller and smaller, as individual decisions led families off in different directions. Ground squirrels were snared as they emerged from their winter dens, and the nests of returning geese, swans, and ducks were robbed of their precious eggs.

By late June or early July the snow was gone and the ocean too treacherous for sledding. The sled had to be cached in some convenient location until the autumn, along with other items too heavy to carry, such as the blubber lamp and the spring tent. Fortunately, the milder weather meant that the far lighter, flimsier summer tent was practical, if not exactly comfortable (particularly against mosquitoes). People carried whatever they needed on their backs, and on the backs of their dogs. They had arrived in the land of summer.

four-and-a-half metres long by three-and-a-half metres wide. Ten or twelve poles supported the central ridge pole, arranged so that although the tent was roughly rectangular the ends were rounded, giving more space and presenting a deflecting surface to the wind. Often the back of the tent was a little higher than the front. The covering was normally made of caribou hide, often spring hides that were unsuitable for any other purpose, and usually arranged so that the hair side was in. About fifteen hides were required for one tent. Occasionally the front part of the tent was depilated, to allow more light into the front living area.

Sometimes, too, a conical tent something like a tipi was substituted. As much as possible the interior arrangements resembled those of a snowhouse, with the sleeping area at the back and the lamp and table at the front.

On reaching the coast people would cache some of their winter gear, preferably on small off-shore islands or on the tops of cliffs, safe from maurauding bears or wolverines. As long as snow remained on the ground there was no hurry to leave

THE SLED

Stored for the summer on some rocky beach, the sled was an inert, soulless thing. For almost nine months of the year, however, it occupied the very heart of Arctic life.

The Inuit employed two types of sled: the railed sled, which sits up above its runners and has a railed enclosure at the back for passengers or gear, and the much simpler flat sled, or *komatik*. In Alaska and the Mackenzie Delta region both were used — the railed sled for general travelling and the flat sled for hauling heavy, bulky loads such as boats or piles of frozen meat. Flat sleds tended to be only a metre or two long, and consisted of little more than a pair of runners to strap under a heavy load.

Among the Copper Inuit and elsewhere in the Eastern and Central Arctic only the flat komatik was used, but it tended to be much longer than the flat sleds used in the West. Copper Inuit sleds were usually between about four-and-a-half and five metres long, and about 70 cen-timetres wide. Netsilik sleds tended to be a bit shorter, while those of the Caribou Inuit were generally a bit longer — perhaps a reflection of the availability of the wood necessary for construction.

Flat sleds were stronger than the railed type, and could take a heavier load. The large komatiks of the Canadian Arctic were used by people who had to move all of their earthly possessions several times a winter. The more settled Inuit of the Western Arctic usually had no such need and preferred the lighter railed sled for general travelling. Copper Inuit komatiks were strong enough to carry almost any weight. Often they were piled so high that they towered above their owners.

A komatik was shaped like a ladder, with two stout parallel boards set on edge forming the runners, connected by a platform of lashed cross-slats. Nails or pegs were never used for joining, since a fully loaded sled travelling over rough ice was subject to immense stress and strain. A lashing of bearded sealskin rope was much stronger and more supple than any rigid form of attachment.

The bottoms of the runners were often shod with bone or antler. To further reduce friction, blocks of peat

As with the komatik of the Eastern and Central Arctic, the Alaskan railed sled was lashed rather than pegged together, to provide greater flexibility. Lighter than a komatik, it still needed to withstand hard usage.

Team hitched in tandem

The woman, in harness, urges the dogs on with her voice

Fish laid end to end are rolled in wet caribou or seal hides. Frozen, they will make serviceable sled runners.

The still unfrozen runners are lashed tight to make them strong.

After the runners are joined with bone and antler cross slats, a shoeing of wet moss is applied to the bottom of the runners and frozen into place. A glaze of pure ice will then be applied to make a nearly frictionless sledding surface.

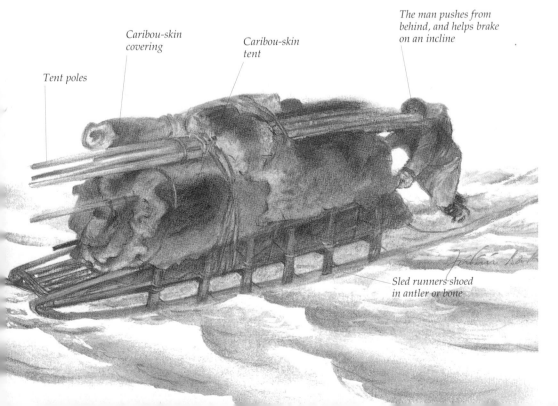

Tent poles

Caribou-skin covering

Caribou-skin tent

The man pushes from behind, and helps brake on an incline

Sled runners shoed in antler or bone

were frozen to the underside of the runners and given a final coating of clear ice. If properly maintained this shoeing could last all winter, and a great deal of care was taken to keep it from chipping or breaking off. Exposed gravel or rocks that might cause damage were cautiously avoided, and halts often called for minor repairs. Snow or ice was melted in a pot and squirted onto the runner by mouth, then smoothed in place with a piece of polar bear skin as it froze. In spring the shoeing was sometimes protected by a skin apron, which acted as a sunshade to keep it from melting.

In the Eastern Arctic sleds were commonly equipped with wooden or antler "up-standers" at the back as an aid to steering and pushing. The Copper Inuit, however, did not drive the sled from behind, and so never used them. Instead, every able-bodied person was in harness helping the dogs pull from the front of the sled.

Not all Inuit had easy access to enough wood to build a sled. The Polar Inuit of northwestern Greenland and the Netsilik of the Queen Maud Gulf area were the most wood-poor, and often had to jury-rig sleds from a variety of materials. They pieced sleds together from antler and bone, and whatever driftwood was available. Runners were sometimes made of fish wrapped in hides that were then soaked and allowed to freeze. Sleds like these are a remark-able testimony to Inuit ingenuity — and they were edible!

Although the Copper Inuit usu-ally had some access to wood, in late spring when the snowcover was poor, or in autumn before people had recovered their cached sleds, they would often improvise with a block of ice, a polar bear skin, or a "poor-man's" sled made of frozen fish and hides.

There were several different ways of hitching the dogs. In Canada most Inuit used a fan hitch, where the dogs pull in an arc, each with its own line to the sled. In Alaska dogs were usu-ally hitched on either side of a single line. Of course when only two or three dogs are involved there is not much difference.

THE TECHNIQUES OF FISHING

Aside from catching fish with their hands, as they sometimes did, the Copper Inuit had two primary fishing techniques: jigging (essentially ice fishing with a hook and line) and spearing. In winter people occasionally jigged for tomcod through the sea ice, but most jigging was done in late spring and early summer through freshwater lake ice, with trout or char the usual catch.

A detached copper side barb and mounting for a trident fish spear

The chief piece of equipment was a barbless copper hook which, having no eye, was set in a bone or antler plug that in turn had a hole for attachment to the fishing line. The line was kept wound up on an antler reel, which doubled as a kind of short fishing pole. Also used were a copper-bladed ice chisel, a small wooden or horn ice scoop, and a bag to hold the fish.

Depending on the thickness of the ice, chopping a fishing hole might take about half an hour. The hook was then baited with a piece of fish skin or some belly flesh and lowered through the hole into the water. Once a suitable depth was reached the hook was kept in a constant up-and-down motion until a strike was made. When this happened the fisherman had to haul back quickly and smoothly on the line to prevent the fish escaping from the barbless hook. This was done either by reeling in the line with a rolling hand-over-hand motion, or simply walking backward until the fish was hauled up onto the ice. It was then killed with a sharp crack on the head and placed on the ice with its head toward the hole. The fishing hole would slowly become surrounded with dead fish, all pointing inward, so that the fisherman was always in the middle of a school of fish.

Not all lakes were equally good for fishing. Some could not support a resident fish population as they were too shallow and froze right to the bottom in winter. Even good fishing lakes had areas to be avoided. When someone found an unusually good spot, he would mark it with two piles of stones on an overlooking ridge.

By early summer the lakes were generally so full of open ponds and shore leads that it was no longer necessary to chop holes in the ice. The hook now acted more like a lure to attract fish into range, where they could be speared. Trident-shaped spears, with three prongs set on the end of a long wooden shaft, were also used in shallow streams when the fish were spawning. The centre prong, which impaled the fish, was flanked on either side by prongs with inward-facing copper barbs on the ends. These side-prongs were very flexible and expanded out to accommodate the fish, while the barbs kept it from wriggling free. This remarkably

Incised mouth

Bone inlaid eye

Cross-hatching imitating scales

Gills

This antler lure is of Thule-culture origin, and about 800 years old.

Wooden side prongs

Leather binding

Sealskin lashing

Barbs

Centre prong

Antler

Copper barb

The flexible side prongs of a trident fish spear open around the fish, which is impaled on the centre prong and held tightly in place by the copper side barbs.

Spring ice fishing through a hole in the ice. The fisherman is bobbing a lure up and down to attract a fish, which he will then attempt to stab with his three-pronged spear.

Fishing with a hook and line was most commonly practised in the spring, both through sea ice and on frozen lakes.

Combination rod and reel

Fishing line made of braided sinew

Copper hook

Antler hook shank with attached lures

efficient style of fish spear was used by Inuit everywhere.

Migrating or spawning fish were often trapped by low stone dams or weirs built across narrow streams. Usually four dams were built at intervals of about 25 metres, the first three with gaps through which the fish could pass, but the last dam blocking the passage completely. When the trap was full everyone — men, women, and children — rushed in with spears, stabbing away as fast as they could and either throwing the fish up on the bank or stringing them on a line through the gills.

In a few locations the fish run was so abundant that no strategems were required. Here gaffs or "fish rakes" were used to simply haul fish right out of the water. Samuel Hearne saw fishing of this sort at Bloody Falls on the lower Coppermine River in 1771. As he described it, the fish (probably char) were so numerous "that when a light pole, armed with a few spikes ... was put under the water, and hauled up with a jerk, it was scarcely possible to miss them."

Just as fish caught by jigging were laid with their heads toward the hole, so fish caught by spearing had to be laid out facing the direction they were going when caught, upstream or downstream. When hung to dry, the same rule had to be observed; in that way the spirit of the fish could continue the spawning run.

In traditional times net fishing was practised only in the Western Arctic. Nets were made of baleen or caribou sinew, with stone sinkers and wood or bark floats. In summer nets were set from boats, or from shore using long, flexible poles. In winter they were set under the ice. Archaeological evidence suggests that net fishing was developed too late in Alaska to have been part of the cultural repertoire of the original Thule Inuit immigrants to Arctic Canada.

SMALL GAME HUNTING

The Copper Inuit never missed an opportunity to capture anything edible, no matter how small. Gulls, jaegers, even song birds were hunted, along with ducks, geese, swans, loons, and a host of small mammals. In early summer, eggs were gathered.

Young boys were often the main hunters, and would spend hours throwing rocks at ptarmigans, or waiting patiently, snare in hand, outside a ground squirrel burrow. Small game was by no means neglected by their fathers or mothers either.

The Copper Inuit hunter was not noticeably successful with many types of small game, particularly birds. Their usual weapon against these animals was the bow and arrow.

Hunting birds with a bow was no easy task, however; it was difficult to get within range, and even harder to hit such a small target. Often a hunter would circle around a flock of ptarmigan, for instance, until several birds were lined up, making it less likely he would miss. Wolves, foxes, and rabbits were also shot with a bow and arrow. Whenever possible the hunter would try to lure them into range by making whistling sounds or somehow attracting their curiosity. Special blunt arrowheads were sometimes used, so that small creature would not be too mangled.

Many other Inuit groups had a much better-developed technology for hunting birds, including bola balls to bring down flying birds, and a special bird spear, with projecting side barbs to give it something of a "shotgun effect." Propelled with a throwing board, usually from a kayak, bird spears could be very effective. In parts of the Eastern Arctic, and especially in northwestern Greenland, nets set on poles were used for catching birds like dovekies, which live in large, dense colonies. Often thousands of these small birds could be taken in a few days.

The Copper Inuit rarely used such weapons, but they did better with traps and snares. Young hunters might wait for hours outside a ground squirrel burrow, trying to snare the animal when it emerged with a noose of plaited sinew. Gulls and other birds were sometimes caught by building small snow structures with a very thin roof. The hunter would place a bit of caribou liver or some other tasty morsel on the roof and crouch inside. When a bird landed to feed, he grabbed its feet through the snow. Foxes and wolves were taken with dead-fall traps, a construction of rocks or ice blocks with a heavy roof supported by a baited stick. When the bait was touched the roof fell on the animal and killed it. Dead-falls were used before the arrival of Europeans, but became particularly common during the early years of the fur-trade period, after a mar-

This light, barbed lance was used for hunting birds from a kayak. It was lauched with a throwing board to increase its range, while the side barbs increasing its effective killing diameter.

Handle

These Yuit bola balls were used to bring down flying birds.

Whale-bone bola balls

Brown lemmings also live in colonies, and maintain extensive but shallow tunnels under the moss. The skins of this small rodent were used to decorate the backs of coats.

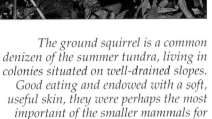

The ground squirrel is a common denizen of the summer tundra, living in colonies situated on well-drained slopes. Good eating and endowed with a soft, useful skin, they were perhaps the most important of the smaller mammals for Copper Inuit hunters.

Arctic hares are unusually large and stay white all summer. More gregarious than most other hares or rabbits, they were still difficult to hunt.

Barbs

Point

ket for fox pelts opened up but before people could buy steel traps. Carnivores were trapped mainly for their hides, but were also eaten.

Many other stratagems were employed. A double-ended bone needle, pierced in the middle by an eye through which a sinew thread was passed, was wrapped in a bit of meat and placed on the shore to attract gulls. Once the gull had swallowed the bait, the hook stuck in its throat and it could not escape. Moulting waterfowl, unable to fly for several weeks in July, were stalked if they strayed from the water, and then run down and throttled. Rabbits were caught in snares set between piles of rock. Slings were improvised, and used for pitching rocks at ducks or ptarmigan.

It was all food for the pot, and good training for the young hunter. In times of plenty, it must have often happened that food offerings like a badly mangled gull were treasured not so much for their intrinsic food value as for what they represented in terms of a young boy's hunting skills. Children learned primarily by doing, and small game hunting was an excellent school.

Big Game Hunting

The principal weapon used for hunting caribou and musk-ox was the bow. Most were made from three pieces of spruce, spliced and lashed to form an implement about 120 centimetres long. Around the eastern end of Coronation Gulf, where wood was comparatively scarce, bows were sometimes made of musk-ox horn instead, cut and riveted into shape.

Because dry spruce has little tensile strength, and horn even less, it was necessary to strengthen the bow with a back lashing of braided sinew. In effect, the bow itself was merely a framework supporting the sinew lashing, which supplied the weapon's real power. This type of bow was typical of most Inuit groups, and once more shows how real technological ingenuity can overcome serious limitations in raw materials.

Most Inuit were indifferent archers. One visitor described an archery contest where an up-turned sod about 30 centimetres square was used as a target. At forty paces only one shot in twenty hit the mark. The Inuit excelled not in archery but in strategy and tactics, in coming close enough to the animal to make sure the arrow hit the mark.

They used a variety of techniques, many of which depended on getting the animal to come to the hunter rather than the other way around. Large cooperative drives involving perhaps twenty or thirty people were the most productive method. A line of shouting, howling women and children would drive a herd of caribou towards an arranged ambush. Topography and wind direction were carefully considered; a successful drive called for both luck and painstaking attention to detail.

There were rarely enough people to drive a herd unaided. For assistance, people often built rows of small stone figures along ridge tops or in other conspicuous locations. Known as *inukshuit* (meaning "like a person"), they were usually very simple constructions of two or three rocks piled one on another, with a sod placed on top, in imitation of a person.

Sometimes walking sticks hung with a coat or small wooden paddles fluttering in the breeze were substituted. Whatever the form, they were generally placed about a dozen paces apart, and functioned "like a person" alarming the caribou and keeping them moving in the right direction.

Somewhere up ahead, the men were waiting in ambush. They might be hidden in shooting pits overlooking the path of the caribou, lying head down with their bows and arrows beside them. As the herd ran by they would stand and shoot, trying to bring down as many animals as possible. Better yet, if kayaks were available the hunters would be waiting at a watercrossing, ready to paddle out after the swimming caribou and lance them. Many, many animals could be killed this way.

Even very small-scale drives were attempted. Two men out hunting might split up upon seeing a small herd or even a single animal. While one got into position downwind the other moved upwind, and by showing himself to the caribou hoped to startle them into bow range of his companion.

A more passive technique involved observing a small herd as it leisurely grazed its way across the tundra. Hunters often climbed high hills to scan the surrounding countryside for this purpose. With an intimate knowledge of caribou behaviour, and keeping in mind topography and wind conditions, it was often possible to anticipate the direction the herd would move, and to

Antler

These arrows are the contents of a single quiver, and display considerable variation in both style and raw material.

With a backing of braided sinew that supplied most of the power, Inuit bows were capable of shooting an arrow right through a caribou at close range.

Braided sinew bow string

Spruce frame

Braided sinew backing

Barb

Raw copper

ambush them. Great patience was often required; hunters might wait hours for approaching caribou to wander within range.

The Inuit were also skilled stalkers. Every trick involving wind direction and cover was used, and when all else failed the hunter resorted to imitation. By drawing his hood over his head, stooping as he walked, and holding his bow and walking stick up like antlers, he could sometimes mislead the caribou into thinking he was one of them. Using this ruse he might be able to get within bow range.

Musk-ox could be comparatively easy to hunt. With the help of dogs they could be rounded up into their characteristic defensive ring. In this position they were fairly invulnerable to attack from arrows (but not rifles), since so much of the target consisted of horn and hair. Dogs, however, could lure an individual musk-ox out of the ring by yapping and barking, and once the hunter had a clear side shot the animal was his.

Hunters used a system of signals to communicate silently in the field. "Caribou or musk-ox in sight" was indicated by alternately throwing up the arms and stooping. If game was near an outstretched hand was lowered toward the ground several times as a sign to keep especially quiet. If the other hunter was some distance away, the person signalling might croak like a raven to get his attention. Grizzly bears required a special signal, and were approached with great caution. Whenever possible they were shot from cover, lest the hunter become the hunted. The grizzly was probably the most feared Arctic animal, but a hunter would be ashamed not to attack.

The Inuit hunter carried his bow in a hide case to protect it from the elements. Attached to the case was a quiver, a small tool kit, and a decorated bone carrying handle.

Tool kit

Handle

Quiver

Bow case

UMIAK HUNTERS

**Most Inuit hunted sea mammals during the summer.
In fact the Inuit in general can be divided into "rich" and "poor"
on the basis of summer access to sea mammals.**

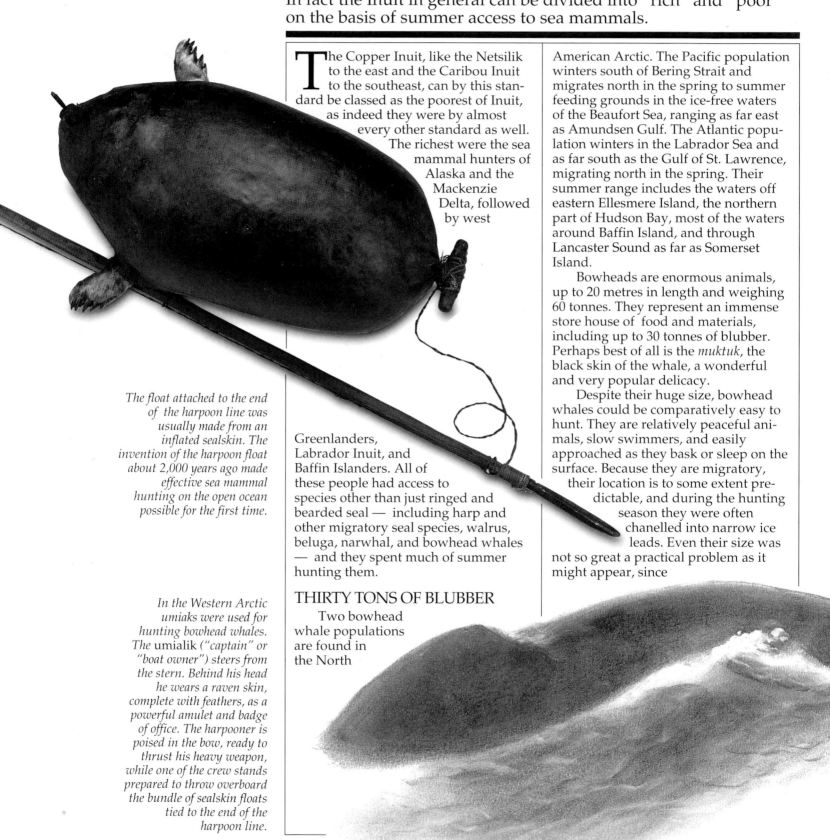

The Copper Inuit, like the Netsilik to the east and the Caribou Inuit to the southeast, can by this standard be classed as the poorest of Inuit, as indeed they were by almost every other standard as well. The richest were the sea mammal hunters of Alaska and the Mackenzie Delta, followed by west

The float attached to the end of the harpoon line was usually made from an inflated sealskin. The invention of the harpoon float about 2,000 years ago made effective sea mammal hunting on the open ocean possible for the first time.

In the Western Arctic umiaks were used for hunting bowhead whales. The umialik *("captain" or "boat owner") steers from the stern. Behind his head he wears a raven skin, complete with feathers, as a powerful amulet and badge of office. The harpooner is poised in the bow, ready to thrust his heavy weapon, while one of the crew stands prepared to throw overboard the bundle of sealskin floats tied to the end of the harpoon line.*

Greenlanders, Labrador Inuit, and Baffin Islanders. All of these people had access to species other than just ringed and bearded seal — including harp and other migratory seal species, walrus, beluga, narwhal, and bowhead whales — and they spent much of summer hunting them.

THIRTY TONS OF BLUBBER

Two bowhead whale populations are found in the North

American Arctic. The Pacific population winters south of Bering Strait and migrates north in the spring to summer feeding grounds in the ice-free waters of the Beaufort Sea, ranging as far east as Amundsen Gulf. The Atlantic population winters in the Labrador Sea and as far south as the Gulf of St. Lawrence, migrating north in the spring. Their summer range includes the waters off eastern Ellesmere Island, the northern part of Hudson Bay, most of the waters around Baffin Island, and through Lancaster Sound as far as Somerset Island.

Bowheads are enormous animals, up to 20 metres in length and weighing 60 tonnes. They represent an immense store house of food and materials, including up to 30 tonnes of blubber. Perhaps best of all is the *muktuk*, the black skin of the whale, a wonderful and very popular delicacy.

Despite their huge size, bowhead whales could be comparatively easy to hunt. They are relatively peaceful animals, slow swimmers, and easily approached as they bask or sleep on the surface. Because they are migratory, their location is to some extent predictable, and during the hunting season they were often chanelled into narrow ice leads. Even their size was not so great a practical problem as it might appear, since

Horn Head-board Stringer Rib Gunwale Seat

Skin covering

Inuit hunters usually selected yearling animals less than half the adult length.

In recent times, most bowhead whaling was done by Western Inuit. In Alaska the spring hunt was the most important, when leads were opening in the ice and the whales began migrating north through Bering Strait to their summering grounds in the Beaufort Sea. Their path sometimes took them near shore where peninsulas jut-ted into the water, and it was in these locations that the large whaling villages of Cape Prince of Wales, Point Hope, and Point Barrow were situated.

A FAST AND ROOMY VESSEL

During the whaling season a close watch was kept

Scale model of an umiak. In the Eastern Arctic they were used mainly for summer transportation.

Harpooner

Bow horn

Graphite face paint

Walrus-hide covering

Labrets

Float

Sternsman

Graphite face paint

Raven skin

Paddler

Steering paddle

127

for whales at all times, and boat crews would put to sea in a large skin boat called an umiak as soon as animals were spotted.

An umiak is an open boat, with a wooden frame and a covering of

Typical examples were about nine or ten metres long, under two metres wide, and about a metre deep. The bottom was flat, with no keel, and both ends were normally pointed. It could be propelled with either oars and paddles, and was described by European sailors as very fast and manoeuvrable.

The umiak was also used in the Eastern Arctic, but almost exclusively as a means of transport. It was the family boat, the "women's boat," in which long summer journeys were made, loaded with weapons and provisions, children, dogs, tents, and clothing. An elder sat in the stern controlling the rudder, while the women rowed, keeping time with songs. Sometimes sails were used, with the mast placed right in the bow. Alongside, the men kept pace in their kayaks. When they landed, the umiak was overturned on the beach and used as a temporary shelter.

A DISCIPLINED HARMONY

In Alaska where the umiak was above all a hunting vessel, its crew was normally composed of men, although women might be drafted to fill any vacancies. A typical whaling crew might number eight paddlers, a sternsman, who was customarily the *umialiq* or boat owner, and the harpooner, who stood in the bow. Once their prey had been sighted and

Carved effigies like this were hung in the bow of the umiak, where they magically helped to charm whales within striking range.

bearded seal or walrus hide. Although comparatively light, it could transport up to thirty people and several tonnes of goods. In the Western Arctic it was used for both travelling and hunting, and tended to be fairly streamlined.

Sculptured whale's tail

Incised whale's tail

the boat put to sea, they approached the animal as silently as possible, trying to keep the waves from slapping against the side of the boat.

The crew was highly disciplined, experienced in the dangerous task before them. They were armed with magic and protected by supernatural forces, prepared by religious ceremonies lasting for several weeks before the hunt. Each man wore new, clean clothing, to show respect for the whale. In the boat were powerful amulets and charms, designed to ensnare the whale and keep it from escaping.

In front of the harpooner lay the whaling harpoon, two-and-a-half metres long and very heavy. Tens of metres of walrus-hide line connected the detachable head of the harpoon with a bundle of inflated sealskin floats. When the whale was struck these floats were thrown overboard as quickly possible, and the harpoon line uncoiled like a hissing snake. The wounded whale was marked and worn down by the heavy drag of the floats, and when it surfaced again the hunters were there ready for it, perhaps joined by other boats from the shore. The whale would be harpooned again. Towing a growing collection of floats, it would begin to tire and eventually became too

exhausted to swim. An umiak would paddle up beside it and the tail flukes would be cut with a lance, making escape impossible. The whale was then lanced to death.

Bowheads were also hunted in the Eastern Arctic, particularly in the Baffin Island area and along the Labrador coast. They were attacked as they were encountered by kayakers, only occasionally assisted by umiak crews. Whaling was less of an organized, systematic pursuit than in the West, and hunting success seems to have been lower. Effective whaling probably requires the heavy whaling harpoon with its great cluster of floats, but this weapon is simply too ungainly to be wielded from a kayak.

Two chipped-stone whale amulets, each about 4 cm long. Harpooners and whaling captains commonly wore amulets like these suspended from headbands during the hunt.

Alaskan Inuit whale-shaped wooden box for storing harpoon blades. A small lid would have held the blades in place. On the reverse side, the whale has been equipped with bits of iron pyrite for eyes.

IN A KAYAK

A kayak is a small, decked-over skin boat, usually designed for a single person. Like an umiak it has a wooden framework, usually of spruce, and a cover, most commonly sealskin.

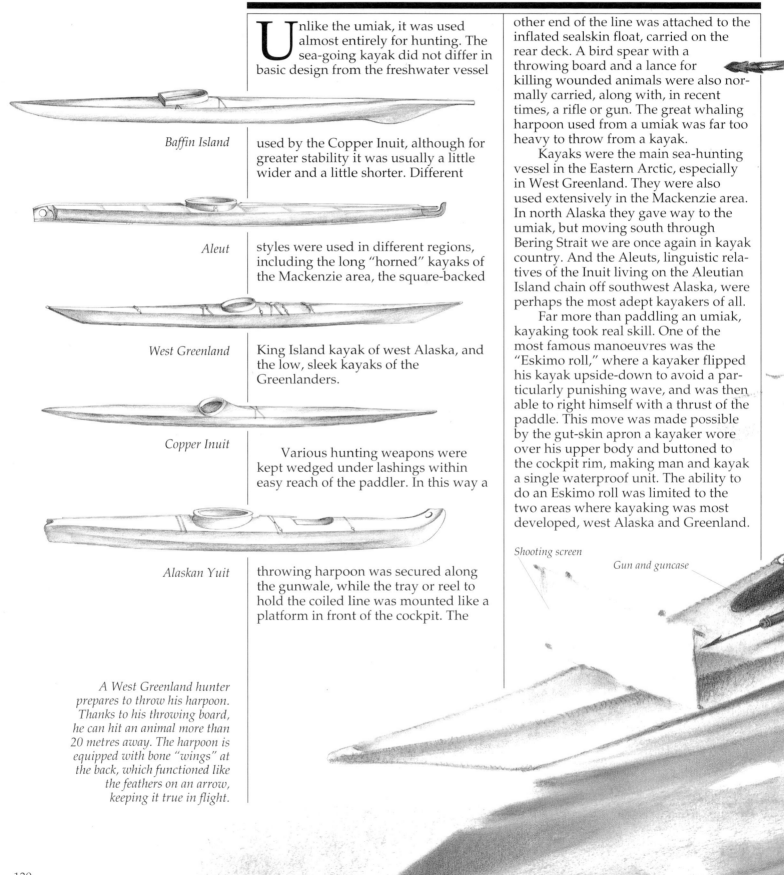

Unlike the umiak, it was used almost entirely for hunting. The sea-going kayak did not differ in basic design from the freshwater vessel

Baffin Island

used by the Copper Inuit, although for greater stability it was usually a little wider and a little shorter. Different

Aleut

styles were used in different regions, including the long "horned" kayaks of the Mackenzie area, the square-backed

West Greenland

King Island kayak of west Alaska, and the low, sleek kayaks of the Greenlanders.

Copper Inuit

Various hunting weapons were kept wedged under lashings within easy reach of the paddler. In this way a

Alaskan Yuit

throwing harpoon was secured along the gunwale, while the tray or reel to hold the coiled line was mounted like a platform in front of the cockpit. The

A West Greenland hunter prepares to throw his harpoon. Thanks to his throwing board, he can hit an animal more than 20 metres away. The harpoon is equipped with bone "wings" at the back, which functioned like the feathers on an arrow, keeping it true in flight.

other end of the line was attached to the inflated sealskin float, carried on the rear deck. A bird spear with a throwing board and a lance for killing wounded animals were also normally carried, along with, in recent times, a rifle or gun. The great whaling harpoon used from a umiak was far too heavy to throw from a kayak.

Kayaks were the main sea-hunting vessel in the Eastern Arctic, especially in West Greenland. They were also used extensively in the Mackenzie area. In north Alaska they gave way to the umiak, but moving south through Bering Strait we are once again in kayak country. And the Aleuts, linguistic relatives of the Inuit living on the Aleutian Island chain off southwest Alaska, were perhaps the most adept kayakers of all.

Far more than paddling an umiak, kayaking took real skill. One of the most famous manoeuvres was the "Eskimo roll," where a kayaker flipped his kayak upside-down to avoid a particularly punishing wave, and was then able to right himself with a thrust of the paddle. This move was made possible by the gut-skin apron a kayaker wore over his upper body and buttoned to the cockpit rim, making man and kayak a single waterproof unit. The ability to do an Eskimo roll was limited to the two areas where kayaking was most developed, west Alaska and Greenland.

Shooting screen

Gun and guncase

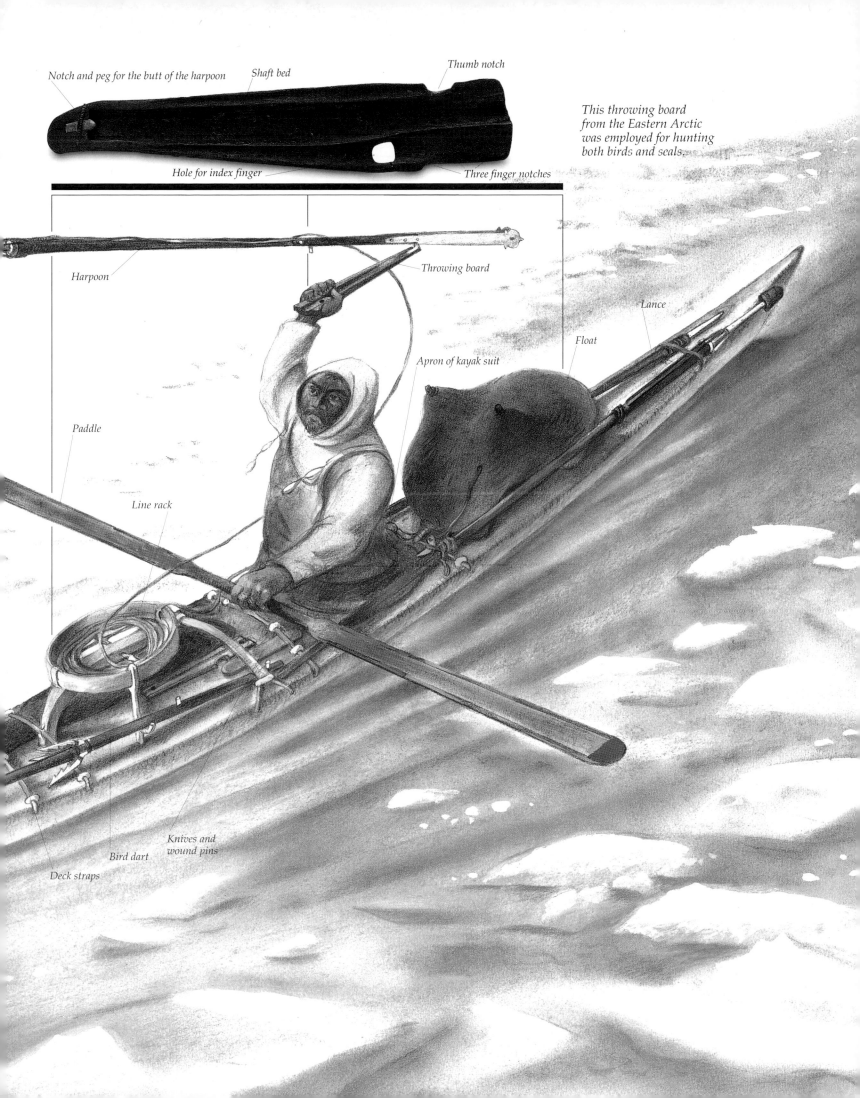

Notch and peg for the butt of the harpoon

Shaft bed

Thumb notch

This throwing board
from the Eastern Arctic
was employed for hunting
both birds and seals.

Hole for index finger

Three finger notches

Harpoon

Throwing board

Lance

Float

Apron of kayak suit

Paddle

Line rack

Knives and
wound pins

Bird dart

Deck straps

In Greenland there was (and is) a psychological condition associated with kayaking called in English or Danish "kayak-angst," and in Greenlandic Inuktitut *nangiarneq*. It consisted of acute anxiety attacks experienced while kayaking, and could ruin a kayaker for life, or even drown him. It typically struck on a hazy, calm day when the sky was perfectly reflected in the glassy water, and the shadow of the kayak could be tracked through the water. The kayaker became completely disoriented, shook violently, experienced acute fear of capsizing, intense dizzi-

shaft is rigidly attached to the rest of the harpoon, and since the harpoon never leaves the hunter's hand there is no danger of breakage. In a throwing harpoon the foreshaft has to be less fragile, and is meant to disengage from the socket on impact to keep it from breaking and to help unseat the toggling head.

Throwing harpoons came in a variety of sizes, depending on the intended prey. Comparatively large, heavy weapons were used for walrus and

ness, and sometimes hallucinations. It is not known why Alaskan kayakers were not afflicted with this malady.

The throwing harpoon used from a kayak comprises a number of parts: a detachable head with a socket in the base, which fits on an ivory or antler foreshaft, which in turn sits in a socket-piece attached to the end of the wooden harpoon shaft. A stabbing harpoon, like that used by the Copper Inuit, has a long narrow foreshaft designed to fit down a seal's breathing hole. This fore-

small whales, while lighter harpoons known as bladder darts were generally employed against seals. A throwing board, essentially a kind of wooden sling that increased the leverage of the throwing arm, was often used to improve the range.

LONG-DISTANCE JOURNEYS

Despite the dangers of rocky coasts and frequent storms, Inuit kayakers were capable of remarkable journeys. Just how remarkable is apparent from a

number of European accounts as early as the 1420s of "Finn-men" or "pygmies" found washed ashore off northern Scotland and Norway in their skin boats. From the descriptions it is obvious that these "Finns" were actually Eastern Arctic Inuit. On several occasions their kayaks were preserved; at one time one hung in the Physicians Hall in Edinburgh, another in a church at Burra, in Orkney, and a third in the cathedral of Nidaros, on the west coast of Norway.

The last and best recorded incident dates to about the year 1700, when a kayaker paddled into the mouth of the River Don, just outside of the town of Aberdeen on the northeast coast of Scotland, and promptly died. His kayak and some of its accessories (harpoon, lance, bird dart, and throwing board) are still housed at the Anthropological Museum of the University of Aberdeen. From their style it is apparent they came from near the modern town of Nuuk, in central West Greenland. Several sightings in the late 1690s suggest that this man might have lived for several years around the outer islands of Orkney before his dying foray up the Don.

How Inuit kayakers managed to survive a transatlantic crossing is not clear. Blown before even the stiffest gale the voyage would take at least nine or ten days; far too long to live without drinking water, and far too long for a skin kayak to remain leak-free and buoyant. Dates as early as 1420 seem to preclude hitching a ride on a European trading vessel. But at whatever personal cost and however inadvertent, voyages of discovery between the Old World and the New were not made in one direction only.

Model kayak, Eastern Arctic. The kayak is one of the most beautiful of watercraft, and can be remarkably seaworthy. Sealskin was the most common covering.

The ribs are mortised in place. The dimensions of a kayak took into account its intended function. Seagoing kayaks were usually broader and more stable than those used on freshwater lakes, where speed was the prime concern.

OTHER PREY

The huge walrus is the most social and gregarious of all sea mammals. In warm weather walrus haul out on rocky beaches to bask in the warm sun.

Walrus were a very important game animal both in Alaska and in the Eastern Arctic, particularly around Iglulik, north of Hudson Bay, and in the St. Lawrence Island region, just south of Bering Strait. The western population is migratory, wintering in the north Pacific. This is less true of the Eastern Arctic population, which undertakes local migrations only when solid ice forms over inshore waters. Walrus are well adapted to fairly dense pack ice and can even keep open breathing holes through thin fast ice, butting it from below with their massive skulls.

INOFFENSIVE ON LAND …

Walrus can be very aggressive, dangerous animals. They are large and powerful — a bull can weigh a tonne and a half — well armed with powerful tusks, and a bellicose personality. Their skin is very thick and hard to penetrate; unless razor-sharp, harpoons tend to bounce off. Most dangerous of all are irritable old males. As with some other large, thick-skinned animals, older males sometimes turn rogue, living violent, lonely lives. Rogue walrus bulls commonly prey on seals and even young narwhal or beluga, and can apparently be identified by their yellow-stained tusks. Otherwise, walrus live primarily on molluscs.

Only when surprised on land, at their hauling-out spots, were they awkward and fairly docile. If cut off from the water, they could be herded and

Weighing over a tonne and armed with fearsome tusks, a walrus can be a very dangerous and aggressive animal. Few hunters dared to attack one from a kayak if the animal was in the water.

killed with spears. They also like to bask in smaller groups on ice flows, where they were harder to hunt. In the water, they were usually considered too dangerous to attack from a boat.

BUT DANGEROUS IN THE WATER

In the Eastern Arctic walrus were commonly hunted from the ice edge. The hunter would try to lure the animal into range by making grunting noises. It was then harpooned and the end of the harpoon line made fast to an ice anchor or frozen block of ice. The experienced hunters would wait a brief instance after the walrus appeared before throwing, for when the walrus turned to dive it exposed its most vulnerable spot, just under the front flippers, where the

skin is comparatively thin. A walrus harpooned there was sometimes killed outright.

Even if not killed immediately, once securely caught the walrus was doomed. Every time it slackened on the harpoon line it was hauled in a little closer to the ice edge, until it could be lanced to death. It was not uncommon, however, for the hunter to become entangled in the line and killed. And sometimes a walrus would attack the hunter from below if he was standing on thin ice. In this situation the wise hunter would dodge a few steps to one side after throwing his harpoon, so that he could lance the animal as it came at him, smashing up through the ice where he had been standing.

Walrus were also stalked as they lay basking on an ice flow, attacked from behind as they slept. Once hit with a harpoon, they sometimes tried to attack the boat. Kayakers in particular were very vulnerable, and usually tried to work in pairs. That way one could come to the rescue of the other, and, while the first hunter was escaping, his partner could try to get a second harpoon into the animal. Instead of attacking a boat the walrus would occasionally restrict his attentions to the float on the end of the harpoon line, ripping it to

Walrus are social creatures, congregating in great numbers at traditional "hauling out" spots. Agile in the water, they are ungainly and helpless on land.

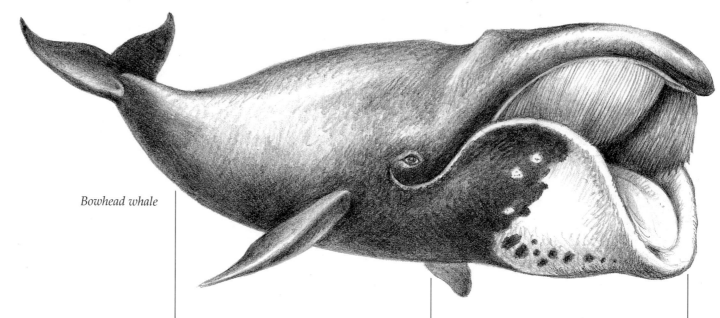

Bowhead whale

pieces with his tusks. Not surprisingly, guns were quickly adopted for this kind of hunting.

Hunting walrus was a very dangerous way to make a living.

A MILDER FOE

The beluga or white whale is the small, toothed whale of the Arctic. They are migratory and fairly gregarious animals, commonly found in pods of from three or four up to several hundred. As with most other large sea mammals, there are distinct Eastern and Western Arctic populations, separated by a Central Arctic into which they rarely venture. Unlike the walrus, they have a mild disposition and rarely if ever attack humans. Belugas have an adult length of four or five metres, and as a result are much easier to hunt than bowheads. Because of its great manoeuvrability the kayak seems to have been the favoured vehicle, and perhaps as a consequence belugas were hunted only casually along the north Alaskan coast. Hunting strategies involved individual stalking through ice flows and cooperative drives where a fleet of perhaps six or eight kayakers would herd a pod of whales into some natural cul de sac, where they could be lanced or harpooned to death.

Narwhal

Beluga

Beluga hunting was particularly important around the mouth of the Mackenzie River. At the village of Kittegazuit up to a thousand people gathered for the beluga hunt from July through September each year, making it perhaps the largest seasonal aggregation on the entire Arctic coast of North America. They took advantage of a natural whale trap formed by the funnel-shaped mouth of the east channel of the river. Several hundred kayakers would go out at a time, forming a long chain across the mouth of the funnel, driving a pod of whales before them with loud cries and splashes. The terrified animals would beach themselves on mud flats, where they could easily be lanced.

Sometimes a pod of belugas would become trapped by encroaching ice in the autumn. Once their escape was cut off it was comparatively easy to harpoon the frightened creatures.

AN ANIMAL OF LEGEND

The darker narwhal is found only in the East, north of Hudson Strait, and is most common in the area around northern Baffin Island. It is about the same size as a beluga, with similar habits, and was also hunted primarily from kayaks. Like the beluga and the bowhead, the skin of the narwhal is the fatty, delicious substance known as *muktuk*. It is eaten raw or frozen, or sometimes fermented in oil, and is one of the most prized of all Arctic foods.

The striking feature of the narwhal is its long, spirally twisted tusk.

A hunter in his kayak and some prey animals

Actually a tooth from the upper jaw that projects through the upper lip, it may attain a length of almost three metres. Its function is unknown, but it is found only on male animals.

With its tusk, the narwhal seems to be one origin of the unicorn myth of medieval Europe. The Norse, who settled in southwestern Greenland beginning in about A.D. 1000 hunted narwhal, and the tusks were traded back to Europe as unicorn horns. Drinking cups were commonly made from them, as they were thought to be proof against poison.

Getting the meat home from the successful hunt of a large animal like a narwhal or walrus was sometimes a problem. Bowhead whales float, and are easily towed, but other large sea mammals do not. Kayak hunters normally made a small incision under the skin of the animal and literally inflated the carcass with air. Umiak hunters had fewer problems, and usually butchered their kill on the spot, since they had a large boat that could be filled.

AN ARCTIC STAPLE

Small seals were hunted nearly everywhere, and it was only in the middle of the Central Arctic that they were ignored in the open-water season. Ice-edge hunting and individual stalking from kayaks were both common techniques, and were much safer employed against seals than against walrus. While the hunting of larger animals was more spectacular, across the Arctic seals were a mainstay of the Inuit diet.

A special type of harpoon, a bladder dart, was often used for hunting seals from a kayak. It was lighter and smaller than other harpoons, and was usually thrown with a throwing-board.

The float, instead of being attached to a harpoon line, was lashed directly to the shaft of the harpoon. It was much smaller than other floats, and was made from the stomach of a gull or loon. Bladder darts had a greater range than other harpoons, perhaps as much as 25 or 30 metres.

One hunting technique used only in the Western Arctic involved sealing with nets, clearly a development from net fishing. Seal nets were made of sinew or baleen, and set in a strategic location with the top edge anchored to the ice and the bottom weighted down with sinkers. They were most effectively operated during the dark days of winter, when swimming seals were unable to see the net hanging in the black water and would quickly become entangled and drown. This was often an extremely productive method of seal hunting. A net could yield a dozen seals in a night, but the work involved — hauling frozen nets in and out of holes in the ice, and disentangling wet seals at -40° C — meant that every kilo of meat was well earned.

Alaskan Inuit believed that in the black of night a strange creature with the head and face of a person and the body of a seal could become entangled in a seal net. The hunter was advised to feel the head of his catch, and if it had long hair he knew it was a "mermaid." Should this happen, the hunter was to lick the palm of his hand and then touch the mermaid. If done properly, he would catch many seals that night. Should he touch the creature without licking his hand, he might be killed.

Walrus

An Alaskan Inuit artist has incised a hunting scene on this ivory boat hook.

Harpooner

Paddler

Sternsman

Whales

Umiak

CHAPTER 8

A BRIEF SEASON OF ABUNDANCE

The cold had returned. Soon it would blanket the land with snow and build vast stretches of ice on the sea for the Kanghiryuarmiut to live on. Most of them had already returned from the tundra and were assembled on the coast. The women had started at once to process the skins for making the winter clothing. They had to work fast; since there was no seal blubber for the lamps, they couldn't work at night. Luckily, they didn't lack for skins, for the caribou had been numerous and generous; they had come from all over to offer themselves to the waiting hunters, as had many foxes, wolverines, and bears.

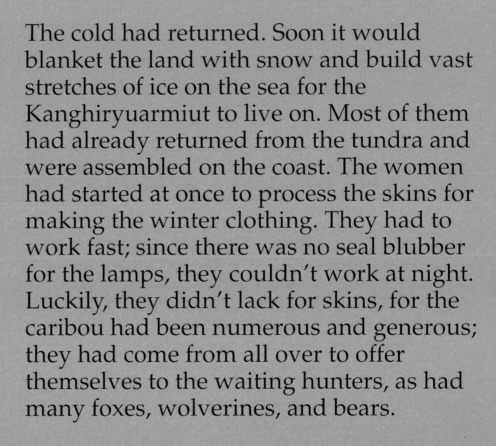

Inuit women sometimes tried to predict the sex of their child before its birth. A boy like that carried by this Quebec Inuit woman was fervently hoped for.

This season of gathering on the coast was perhaps the only period when Akuluk and Tavlo were in total agreement: it was fun. Everyone was busy — the women sewed and the men repaired tools, weapons, sleds, and dog harnesses — but at the same time, everyone was in a festive mood, for all of Kanghiryuak was finally together in one place again, poised between the tundra and the sea ice, waiting for the two worlds to once more blend into one. It was a time for telling stories about what they had seen and done during the summer and preparing to face the long night.

For the first time in her life, Kahina had to sew by herself the clothes that would be worn all winter — trousers, coats, boots — and make sure they were well fitted, solid, comfortable. But although she knew every secret of the seamstress — how to cut and soften the skins, how to prepare the caribou-sinew threads, how to do the hemstitch and whipstitch, how to slide the blind stitch into the hides — something was missing: the calm assurance of her mother when she did her work. Neither Nik nor Agara gave her the same feeling of confidence in her sewing. Her uncertainty showed in her work — something wasn't right. The clothes she made Akuluk try on didn't fit properly. Some places were too tight, while others were too loose. Her friends tried to reassure her, saying the garments would fit better after they had been worn for a while and become completely soft. Still, Akuluk was obviously displeased. Kahina told herself that he was thinking about finding another wife, but she didn't cry. Her mother had often told her that nothing made a man angrier than a woman's tears.

Instead, she thought about how her life would have changed the next time she saw the

What impressed visitors like Diamond Jenness the most about the Copper Inuit was their friendly cheerfulness, their infectious good humour even in the face of hardship and adversity.

Children were often breast-fed until the age of three or four, or even longer. A pure meat diet offered few substitutes for mother's milk.

coast. She would be carrying a child under her coat who would be her pride and joy. Every day, Kahina wondered if she would have a boy or a girl. Nik believed there were signs that could tell, but she didn't know what they were. She thought Kahina's child would be born in the middle of the winter, like the one she herself had lost. If there was no famine, it was a good time to bring a child into the world, better than spring or summer, when there was so much walking to do, sometimes in difficult conditions. In winter the young mother could stay warm in the snowhouse to nurse her baby.

But even if everything went well, even if the child was born during the best seal hunt ever seen, Akuluk certainly would not be happy if his wife gave him a daughter.

Akuluk was feeling a bit disgruntled. Because there had been so few sealskins, he hadn't been able to build the kayak he had been dreaming of for a long time. He had gone to Akilinik last winter not only to see a little of the world and to find himself a good wife, but also to gather enough good wood to build the frame for his kayak.

Why a kayak? Tavlo asked. To hunt caribou at their fording places on the lakes and rivers, Akuluk answered. But what he really wanted was the pleasure of building this boat, more than the pleasure of using it. Making his sled in Akilinik had brought

him great joy; building a kayak would make him even happier. He liked to make things with his hands more than he liked hunting, and definitely more than he liked walking on the tundra in the summer.

Tavlo, who didn't like water, said that a Kanghiryuak hunter didn't need a kayak to survive; in fact, very few had one. He said that it was a useless, fragile toy, which could be used for only a few days during the summer. Akuluk argued that when one had the chance, one must try new things. Working hard was important, but it was not enough: life could only get better — easier — by making improvements in the old ways.

Tavlo didn't want to believe this. He didn't want to change anything about the way they lived. He believed they would never live better than their father had and he was sure that his son, Kunana, would do the same things, at the same times, in the same places.

Before venturing onto the ice once again, Akuluk cached his wood on the coast. Next year, the year after, someday, he would build a kayak. He knew that without the help of his father, for whom no construction had held any secrets, the project would be difficult and complicated, but he would manage. He was sure of it.

THE WORK OF SUMMER

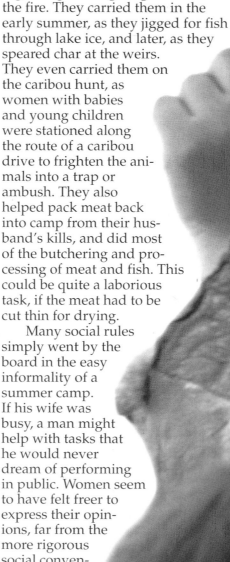

Summer camps were normally pitched on high ground, affording a good view and taking advantage of any wind to keep the insect hordes at bay. The summer tundra abounds in lakes and sloughs, so water for drinking and cooking was never a problem. The sun shone twenty-four hours a day, and life was lived without a schedule.

This toy top was spun with a sealskin cord.

People ate when they were hungry and slept when they were tired, which was not often. Younger children had to be watched, often by a older sister, but children above the age of five or six ran around in almost complete freedom, eating, sleeping, and playing as they wished. Camps were moved every other day or so, depending on whim and the luck of the hunt. Groups constantly formed and re-formed, as individual families wandered off on their own, joining other friends and relatives by chance or purpose at some new lake just over the horizon.

Because of weight problems the summer tent was small and not particularly weatherproof: just half a dozen hides sewed together and held up with walking sticks. Cooking was done in a soapstone boiling pot over an open heather fire, and meals tended to be communal, usually eaten outdoors. On short overnight trips people would often not bother with lugging heavy gear around at all, sleeping in the open air and eating their food raw.

The men spent a great deal of time hunting and fishing, bringing back everything from ground squirrels to caribou for the cooking pot. Living was hand-to-mouth, in the sense that very little food was or could be carried from one camp to another. Instead, any surplus was dried and cached under heavy piles of rock, to be retrieved in the autumn when the sledging season returned. The men hunted hard in a real effort to put up as much food as possible.

Women, too, had many tasks. Very young children required constant care. During the frequent camp moves, mothers carried their babies on their backs, and both fathers and mothers often carried younger children on their shoulders, often perched above a load of sleeping skins, or the folded summer tent. In summer, children too young to walk easily on their own were — literally — a great burden, and a family could not care for more than one or, at most, two at a time.

Mothers continued to carry their babies as they performed their many camp chores: pitching the tent, cooking, and gathering twigs and moss for the fire. They carried them in the early summer, as they jigged for fish through lake ice, and later, as they speared char at the weirs. They even carried them on the caribou hunt, as women with babies and young children were stationed along the route of a caribou drive to frighten the animals into a trap or ambush. They also helped pack meat back into camp from their husband's kills, and did most of the butchering and processing of meat and fish. This could be quite a laborious task, if the meat had to be cut thin for drying.

Many social rules simply went by the board in the easy informality of a summer camp. If his wife was busy, a man might help with tasks that he would never dream of performing in public. Women seem to have felt freer to express their opinions, far from the more rigorous social conventions of the winter village.

The child peeking out from his mother's hood rarely left the safety of her warm back. From this secure perch he was able to peacefully observe the world he would one day have to master.

In the evenings, or when the weather was poor, the men repaired their hunting equipment and women sewed and repaired clothing. When not working, the men might set up sod blocks for an archery contest, or play tag with their children.

When the weather was warm children, especially, often went swimming in shallow lakes and ponds. People were usually in good spirits, and loved to talk and play. In many ways, summer was the richest and fullest time of the year.

An entry from the diary of Diamond Jenness, an early guest of the Copper Inuit, communicates the timeless quality of summer life.

"July 3: Two causes brought about a further division in our little party. The first was the probability of finding caribou farther east, the second the apparent abundance of fish in a certain lake to the north. Accordingly Ikpakhuak and his family went east, while Avranna and his wife, with Kanneyuk, went north. Higilak and Haugak were left to transfer all our things to Lake Kullalluk, some four miles away, while Ikpakhuak and I went hunting. We secured two does and two fawns, an eider duck, a ptarmigan and two lake trout before reaching camp again at one o'clock in the morning. A light south breeze was blowing and the weather was warm and clear, so Higilak left our tent behind at the old camp. During the next three days … we slept in the open."

CHILDBIRTH

A pregnant woman always regarded the future with some apprehension. Where and when would she give birth? In the comfort of her own tent or snowhouse, or in some freezing, temporary structure, thrown up in the middle of a famine or forced migration? Would she have a girl who might have to be abandoned, or a boy who could grow up big and strong, to take care of her when she was old? Would she live or die?

While these worries were inevitable, a Copper Inuit woman did not normally give birth alone. Except in an emergency, she was helped by her husband and by one or two older women who acted as midwives. If the birth was not going well another specialist, the shaman, might be called in to intercede with the spirits. The woman lay on the platform of the snowhouse or floor of the tent, leaning for support on one of the midwives for most of the labour. If help was needed during the pushing stage, the midwife would hold her around the body and try to squeeze the baby out. Otherwise, there was as little interference as possible, since it was believed that a baby should be strong enough to be born on its own.

The woman usually gave birth in a kneeling position. Afterwards, she was expected to do little or no work for a few days, and stayed indoors resting. Children were typically not allowed into the house until this rest period was over, but were sent to stay with friends or relatives. Adults commonly came calling, however, to visit and see how mother and child were doing. A period of sexual abstinence was also usual.

This was the ideal, and the norm. But if by bad luck a woman gave birth on the trail, it might not be possible for the group to stop and wait while all these events happened. Then the woman might have to stay behind, perhaps with her husband or a midwife, to give birth as quickly as she could and then attempt to catch up. If at all feasible, the new mother would be allowed to ride on the sled, keeping her baby warm in her coat. If the child were born during a period of starvation, it would often be killed without delay, no matter how welcome it might otherwise have been.

A starving woman has no milk for a new baby.

Several rituals were observed after a successful birth. The mother had to make a fire under the cooking pot as soon after the birth as possible, so that the child might learn to walk at an early age. The child would be massaged or "worked" by a relative or close friend of the family to ensure various desirable qualities. His legs would be gently stretched to make certain that he would grow tall, his arms pulled so that he would be strong, and so on. Newborn puppies were worked in a similar but rougher fashion. If the child were especially welcomed, a magical song of blessing was composed in celebration of the birth. All who helped in the birth were afterwards considered to be like godparents to the baby.

There were also a few taboos and rituals that had to be observed for longer periods. Whenever a woman with a new baby was about to eat, she was required to cut off a small piece of meat and rub it against the baby's mouth so that the child would never want for food. For some time after the birth, the mother was not allowed to eat or drink from the common pot, but had to use her own cooking pot and bowl. The pot in which her food was cooked must not be given away or traded until the child was grown. In a similar way the child's first garment — a kind of caribou-skin robe open at the front — must be carefully saved while the child was growing. These items were thought to embody the child's health and physical vigour; should they become lost, the child could sicken and die. The umbilical cord might also be kept as an amulet.

None of these events — birth, the cutting of the umbilical cord, first nursing — was associated with a particular ceremony. Nevertheless, the

This painting of a woman in labour was inspired by a black-and-white photograph taken by Richard Harrington, who visited the Caribou Inuit during a serious famine in 1949. Badly weakened by hunger and cold, she is bringing her child into a very difficult world. The photographer never learned whether mother or child survived.

community remembered the particulars of all births: who was present, what the weather was like, whether the dogs were howling or a blizzard blowing. These details would be organized into a story — that individual's personal legend.

Most Inuit named a new baby immediately after birth, or at least after the decision to keep it had been made. But as in so many other things, the Copper Inuit were fairly casual in this regard, often not naming the child for days. Names were suggested by friends and relatives, but the parents had the final say. There was usually little choice, for it was customary throughout the Inuit world to name a child after a recently deceased relative. Normally all of the names associated with that person descended to the child regardless of sex, since traditional names have no gender.

Most people had two names. These were two separate names — not a first and last name — and a person could go by either one. Sometimes family members would use one name and outsiders another, and their relative

Most teaching was by example, and children had plenty of opportunity to see their parents at work.

popularity could wax and wane over the years. People occasionally acquired nicknames that could completely supplant their proper names in general use. Some examples include Kingalokanna, "Big Nose," or Itigaitok, "Footless," a name given to a man who had lost his feet because of freezing.

Proper names too usually had specific meanings, for instance, Kanneyuq, "Sea Scorpion," or Qunualuq, "The Smiling One." But these meanings did not normally come to mind, any more than people now think of flour when addressing someone whose last name is Miller. Thus some Inuit happily bore names that might otherwise have been considered impossibly insulting, such as Minujuk, "The Dirty One," or Anaviluk, "The True Turd."

The lack of concern shown by most Copper Inuit about naming newborns immediately is reflected in their casual attitude towards names in general. Most Inuit thought of the name and the soul as being somehow related. It was sometimes taboo, for instance, to mention the names of the dead. More importantly, the majority of Inuit believed that the dead were somehow reincarnated in newborn babies named after them. The Copper Inuit believed none of these things. For them, as for us, a name was just a name.

A CHILD'S WARDROBE

Aside from a caribou-skin diaper, babies generally went naked. Much of their first few weeks and months were spent under their mother's coat, safe and warm against her skin. In very cold weather, she might add mittens, socks, shoes, and a hood, or wrap a square of fur around the baby's back, held in place with a sinew cord. The baby's front needed no covering, as it rested directly against the mother's bare back.

Traditional Inuit names were almost always inherited from a recently deceased relative. Since name and soul were somehow linked, many Inuit believed that a newborn baby was literally a reincarnation of his or her namesake. A child might thus be its own grandfather.

In a tent or snowhouse the baby slept and played on the sleeping platform, bundled up in caribou-skin blankets if the weather was cold. In summer, the mother would often cover her baby's face with a skin or fan her with a bird's wing to keep off the mosquitoes.

The child did not receive its first real garment until it was old enough to walk, almost always a one-piece suit with a hood, and a flap in the back for easy diaper changing. It was rarely decorated. The mittens attached to the coat were only half sewn on, so that the baby could take its hands out to nurse or play. Seal-skin shoes completed the costume, which of course could be doubled to two layers in cold weather.

Young children's clothing was usually made of caribou skin, often from the complete skin of a caribou calf. The hood was fashioned from the head of the animal, complete with ears and antler buds, the trousers from the legs, and so on. This association between the anatomy of the caribou and that of the child implied a symbolic, magical relationship similar to that suggested by some items of men's clothing.

Ground squirrel skin was also commonly used for children's clothing, since it is extremely soft, sheds very little, and does not mildew quickly when wet (a very practical consideration). It was all the more available, since when worn by a man, ground squirrel skin clothing suggested poor caribou-hunting abilities.

At about five or six years of age, the child's clothing style changed again. Now the outfit was more similar to that of adults, with a separate coat and trousers. Trousers and boots were often in one piece, however, and young girls did not wear the large "hip-wader" boots of adult women. Girls' coats were not very different from those of boys, except that the shoulders were often wider, like those on the coats worn by their mothers. For both boys and girls the bottom of the coat was generally cut straight and fairly short, without the long tails of adult coats. For the most part, decoration was minimal, without chest panels or other colourful inlays. In cold weather a one-piece inner garment was occasionally worn.

Girls sometimes wore their childhood clothes until they married. Boys, on the other hand, began to wear men's styles when they entered adolescence and began actively hunting

and fishing with their fathers. In fact, both sexes crossed the sartorial threshold into adulthood at about the same age, since girls commonly married early, sometimes even before first menstruation.

Like hunters, children were among the most spiritually vulnerable members of society. They generally wore amulets for protection, or as spiritual assistance for their future career, such as a flipper bone from a ringed seal (to make a good caribou hunter) or a piece of fish skin (to make an accomplished seamstress). This was less true among the Copper Inuit than among some of their neighbours. One little Netsilik boy named Tertaq wore eighty amulets sewed to his clothing, including hair from an old man (to give long life), a raven

skin (to make him unseen when hunting caribou), and the head of a red-throated loon (to give luck in fishing). The position where an amulet was worn had an effect on its powers. Most were attached to the inner coat, often to the back. The coat of Tertaq was so covered by amulets as to be practically invisible.

Boys often let their hair grow long as another form of spiritual protection. One boy, who was nearly killed in an accident, never had another haircut again. Among some groups, a child whose brothers and sisters had all died through disease or accident would be dressed in the clothing of the opposite sex, as a way of hiding it from malicious spirits. Clothing was a protection against both physical and spiritual dangers.

A Time to be Carefree

A baby received all of the care and attention her parents could lavish on her. She slept beside her mother on the sleeping platform and was carried everywhere, snug beneath her mother's heavy coat. She was breast-fed on demand, and comforted when she cried. Fathers too delighted in babies. Childhood might be fraught with dangers, but a baby was coddled and cherished by all.

With a pure meat diet there were few substitutes for mother's milk, so weaning was usually a long, slow process, not completed until the child was three or four years old. Broth and boiled fish could be fed to a child at a comparatively young age. Tougher meats like caribou or seal were pre-chewed by a parent.

But fussed over and doted on as infants were, casual visitors sometimes had the impression that older children were badly cared for. Particularly in summer their clothing was often scruffy and in poor repair, and they were allowed to "run wild" without much supervision. They showed little outward respect for their elders, interrupting them, addressing them as equals, and even calling them names. Many Victorian-era explorers, and particularly the missionaries who followed in their wake, clucked their tongues over Inuit child-rearing practices. For it was well known that the Inuit did not beat their children. No wonder they were so spoiled!

To the modern reader, traditional Inuit child-rearing practices seem more reasonable and familiar than they did to Victorian audiences in Europe or North America. Inuit children were actually very well looked after; standards were simply a little more informal than those of middle-class European or American households three or four generations ago. Parents were busy. Clothes were difficult to replace, and those worn were not necessarily the best the child owned. Generally too the virtues of corporal punishment are less apparent now than they were a hundred years ago. And as for running wild, what harm could it do? What trouble could a child get into in a camp or village where he or she was known by everyone?

Even if they were not always respectful, Inuit children were usually very obedient. They were well taught, not with blows but with words, and not always kind words. Inuit culture put a premium on correct behaviour, particularly on cheerful self-control. Disobedience, laziness, and temper

During the endless day of summer, there were few rules — and no bedtime. Boys generally had a little more freedom than girls, who were sometimes saddled with the care of a baby.

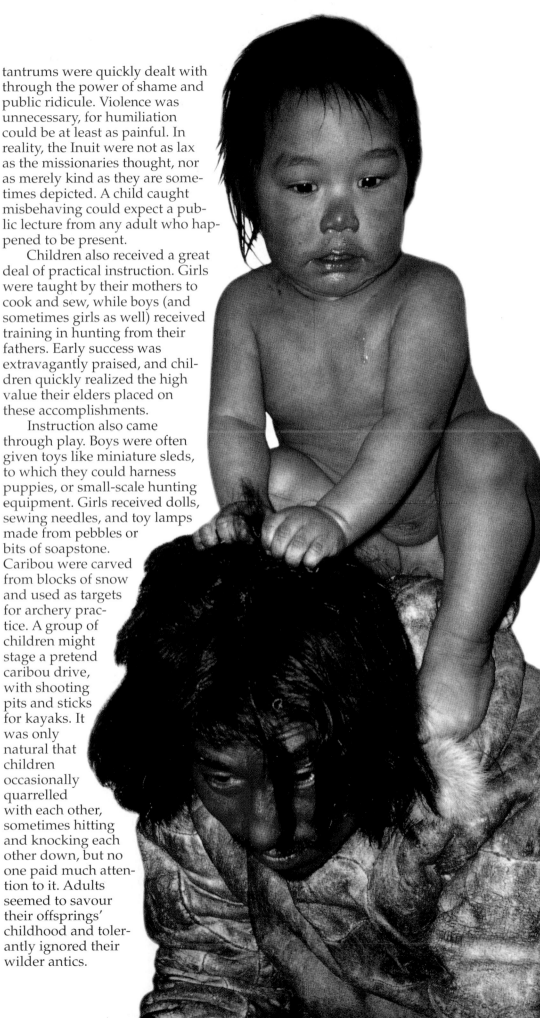

Younger children, especially, were doted on, and it was widely believed that the insult of physical punishment could seriously harm a child's spirit. Victorian explorers often disapproved.

tantrums were quickly dealt with through the power of shame and public ridicule. Violence was unnecessary, for humiliation could be at least as painful. In reality, the Inuit were not as lax as the missionaries thought, nor as merely kind as they are sometimes depicted. A child caught misbehaving could expect a public lecture from any adult who happened to be present.

Children also received a great deal of practical instruction. Girls were taught by their mothers to cook and sew, while boys (and sometimes girls as well) received training in hunting from their fathers. Early success was extravagantly praised, and children quickly realized the high value their elders placed on these accomplishments.

Instruction also came through play. Boys were often given toys like miniature sleds, to which they could harness puppies, or small-scale hunting equipment. Girls received dolls, sewing needles, and toy lamps made from pebbles or bits of soapstone. Caribou were carved from blocks of snow and used as targets for archery practice. A group of children might stage a pretend caribou drive, with shooting pits and sticks for kayaks. It was only natural that children occasionally quarrelled with each other, sometimes hitting and knocking each other down, but no one paid much attention to it. Adults seemed to savour their offsprings' childhood and tolerantly ignored their wilder antics.

Doll, in winter dress, from the Eastern Arctic

A toy kayak from Greenland. The weapons and equipment are made to scale.

GAMES AND TOYS

The Inuit like games. Some were played mainly by children, but adults would join in as the mood took them. Many required no equipment whatsoever. A popular indoor game involved a silence competition; someone, usually a child, would give the signal and everyone had to keep perfectly silent. The first to speak was greeted with roars of laughter.

In the game of "raven," one child was made the hunter, while the others ran off flapping their arms and croaking like ravens. The game was much like tag, and whoever was caught first became the next hunter. Although primarily a children's game, "raven" was also popular among adults during winter camp moves, to keep the blood circulating during halts on the trail. Middle-aged, respected hunters and frail old women would happily join in, flapping their arms and laughing like six-year-olds.

Another familiar game was a version of hide-and-seek. Half the children formed a ring, shielding their eyes or staring at the ground, while the other half ran and hid. When they were hidden they gave a signal. They were then sought out and captured, and in turn became the seekers.

Many games trained children in the skills necessary for adult life, particularly hand-eye coordination games. A popular game called for a willow hoop about 35 centimetres in diameter to be rolled along the ground or thrown into the air. The object was to transfix it with a stick thrown like a spear.

Ajagak, a cup-and-pin game played across the Arctic, normally used the upper arm bone (humerus) of a large bearded seal. A string was attached at one end to the bone and at the other to a bone or antler pin about the size of a pencil. Holding the pin in one hand, the player swung the humerus half a revolution on its string, then impaled it on the peg through one of several drilled holes. Winning meant accomplishing this ten times in a row — once for each finger — all the while keeping count

Skin

Wood

Wood

Parents enjoyed making toys for their children, such as these wood and animal-skin dolls from the Eastern Arctic. The doll would normally be carved by the father, but the mother was assigned the more time-consuming task of sewing the clothing.

The making of string figures was one of the most popular winter pastimes.

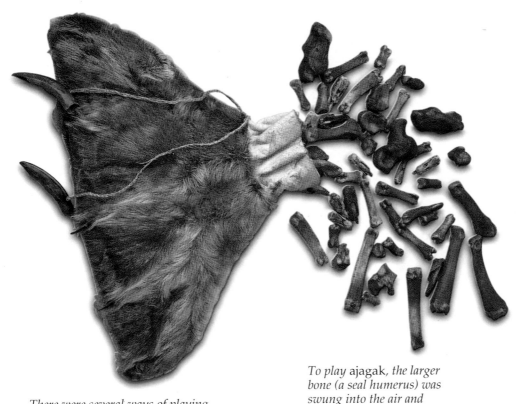

There were several ways of playing the seal bone game. A loop made of sinew could be inserted into the bag, with the object of pulling more bones out than the other players. Or the bones could be tossed like dice; any bone which fell upside down lost.

To play ajagak, *the larger bone (a seal humerus) was swung into the air and impaled in a drilled hole with the bone pin.*

Seal humerus

Drilled hole

Bone pin

by chanting "thumb, one finger, two fingers," and so on. To a beginner it seems practically impossible.

A favourite game in the Eastern Arctic known as *nugluak* was introduced to the Copper Inuit in the spring of 1916 by Netsilik from the Back River area. A short, flat bone plate 5 or 6 centimetres long was made fast by cords to the roof of the house or tent and to a large stone on the floor, so that it was suspended taut about 60 centimetres from the ground. A small hole had been drilled through the middle of the plate, and the players, sitting around in a circle, tried to push small darts or spears through the hole. With everyone stabbing at once, the darts rattled together and pushed each other away, and the plate vibrated wildly. Several minutes often passed before someone was successful.

Most games were played primarily in winter, when there were many people to participate and time often hung heavy during the long evenings. Cat's cradle, like the hoop-and-stick game, could be played only at this time of year. A loop of string twisted into various forms on the player's fingers created dozens of recognized figures, some extremely elaborate. The game was played by most Inuit and some of the figures were recognized across the entire Arctic coast, including one called "the two brown bears," and another called "man carrying a kayak."

Acrobatic feats were practised in the winter dance house. A stout line of bearded sealskin was passed through two holes in the roof and anchored outside with wooden toggles. The acrobat hung by the hands on this line and did various flips for the approval of the watching crowd.

To win, an ajagak *player had to "catch" the humerus ten times in a row, while calling out the count, "one finger, two fingers ..."*

151

THE SOUND OF THE DRUM

The role of celebration in Copper Inuit life can be judged by the importance given to dance partnerships, the third kind of formal partnership (along with spouse exchange and food sharing) that held Copper Inuit society together.

People normally celebrated the arrival of friendly visitors with a drum dance, held in a large snow dance house. On these occasions, hosts and guests usually formed dance partnerships, if they had not already done so on an earlier visit. Dance partners had the honour of dancing before or after each other, a seemingly trivial matter but one of great social importance. Like all partnerships, dance partnerships were normally for life. Without involving the intimacy of a wife exchange, they ensured that both parties would receive a dance of welcome and hospitable entertainment when visiting or travelling.

The drum dance, an expression of community solidarity, was the only form of public celebration among the Copper Inuit. One could be called at any time, but especially to honour the arrival of visitors. Most dances took place in winter, when the large snow dance house was built especially for the purpose, the community was large, and people's best dance clothes were not packed away. At other seasons they improvised as best they could.

The only musical instrument used was a flat, tambourine-like drum, made from a hoop of wood across which was stretched a membrane of de-haired caribou hide. It was struck with a stout stick on the rim only, first on one side and then with a flip of the wrist on the other. Drumming was accompanied by a chanted song, sometimes traditional, sometimes improvised or made up for the occasion, but usually with a familiar tune. Except for children's ditties, all songs were dance songs. They were divided into two classes: *atun* and *pisik*. With a *pisik* the drummer/singer was also the dancer, while in an *atun* the drum might be dispensed with altogether or beaten by someone other than the dancer. In both cases the audience participated in the singing, while the dancer executed a kind of jig in the centre of the ring.

Anyone could lead a dance — man or woman — and people took turns. The drummer began with a few beats on the drum, as though testing it, and then waved it up and down with both hands as a signal that the dance was about to begin. The audience joined in as they recognized the words, and when everything was underway the dancer would begin, swaying her hips and moving around the circle. She might call on her audience to sing louder, especially if the song was new and not much appreciated. In turn, the audience might demand something better liked or more familiar.

Games of tag and "guess who" were played mainly by children, but even respected hunters might join in.

152

The Copper Inuit learned the very popular game of nugluak *from their Netsilik neighbours.*

Skin

Drumstick

Wood

The drum was the only musical instrument known to most Inuit. It was used in drum dances to accompany a traditional or newly composed song.

If things were going well, people would shout encouragements to the dancer, who would respond with wild whoops of joy.

Success on the dance floor was greatly esteemed, particularly for a successful new composition. Some were better poets than others. The explorer Knud Rasmussen, himself part-Inuit and fluent in the Inuit language, judged that the Copper Inuit of Umingmaktok (modern Bay Chimo), at Bathurst Inlet, were the most accomplished poets he met on his entire sled trip from Greenland to Bering Strait, made in the early 1920s. The following dance song was composed by Ipakhuak, a respected Victoria Island hunter.

Here I stand, humble, with outstretched arms.
For the spirit of the air
Lets glorious food sink down to me.

Here I stand, surrounded with great joy.
For a caribou bull with high antlers
Recklessly exposed his flanks to me.
Oh, how I had to crouch, in my hiding place.

The drum dance was common to the entire Inuit world. Alaska also had the Messenger Feast, as jovial in outward appearance, but sometimes a matter of high politics, since it had to do with relationships between the powerful whaling captains known as *umialit*. Their power was based largely on skill and generosity, and their ability to maintain and reward a crew. When an *umialik* wanted to organize a party, he sent a messenger to his peers to invite them and their crews to a sumptuous feast.

The idea was to impress the other crews and intimidate the other *umialit* by the lavishness of the entertainment, and by burying them under mountains of gifts. A return invitation was expected, and the host had to be able to supply food and gifts at least equal to what he had received. His status and success depended on how he handled this situation. If an *umialik* could not reciprocate, he would be humiliated, and would rapidly lose his prestige and standing.

The Messenger Feast also served to distribute food and other items to the entire community. Goods circulated around the *umialit*, who, as owners of the boats and captains of the whaling crews, received a great deal of the take. The Copper Inuit did not indulge in this type of festivity, since they lacked the riches as well as the clearly defined social hierarchy it supported.

THE END OF A WORLD

Before Columbus, iron was already known and prized throughout the Arctic for its hardness and cutting abilities. Asian iron was first traded across Bering Strait almost 2,000 years ago.

By the middle of the Thule period 700 or 800 years ago, tiny bits of iron from one source or another were to be found in tool kits across the entire Arctic coast. It was certainly the most sought-after, long-distance trade item.

Copper was also traded, but more locally. There is some Alaskan copper, but in Canada the sole source was found in Copper Inuit territory. Traded to neighbouring groups to the east and west, it was less valuable than iron because it is so much softer.

Other raw materials were also desirable. A jade-like nephrite used for adze blades was traded from western Alaska at least as far as the Mackenzie River. Amber from the Western Arctic and from northern Ellesmere Island appears sporadically in archaeological sites throughout the Arctic, mainly in the form of beads. Copper Inuit soapstone, as we shall see, had a very wide currency.

IDEAS AND COMMODITIES

Most of this early trade was small in scale and based on low bulk, durable items that passed from hand to hand and from village to village across the top of North America. If in the end immense distances were covered, it was probably slowly, step by step. Nevertheless, trade was not unimportant. In any society trade exerts an influence far beyond the mere commodities exchanged, and the Inuit were no exception. Trade stimulated the growth of important social networks between groups who might otherwise never have met. Along with materials went ideas and information, clothing styles, stories, games, even vocabulary, all facilitated by a basic common language and the comparative ease of transportation in the North. Trade and all that went with it was one of the major factors that held Inuit culture together and gave it a unified face across the immense distances of the Arctic.

Food and animal products also figured in the network, but because of weight and bulk the distances involved tended to be shorter than those associated with commerce in durable raw materials such as iron or nephrite. In north Alaska and in the Mackenzie Delta region, trade in animal products made some real regional economic specialization possible. People living inland could concentrate on caribou hunting, and trade for the blubber they needed for their lamps. Coastal people could hunt sea mammals over the crucial September caribou-hunting season knowing the hides they needed for clothing could be obtained elsewhere. This kind of symbiotic relationship was not possible under the simpler economic regimes of the Central Arctic.

THE FOREIGNERS ARRIVE

The medieval Norse were the first Europeans to trade with Arctic Inuit, and it was primarily animal products that interested them: walrus hide for ropes, ivory, narwhal tusks, and even live polar bears destined for European menageries. Some of these they could obtain for themselves, but there seems to have been a lively exchange with Inuit hunters, who were far more successful. The Inuit appear to have been interested chiefly in iron, and Norse metal has been found in Inuit archaeological sites as far west as the western coast of Hudson Bay. The arm of a Norse trader's balance found in an Inuit site on Ellesmere Island hints of Norse travels into the Canadian Arctic. Another Inuit site on Ellesmere Island

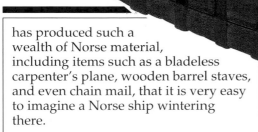

has produced such a wealth of Norse material, including items such as a bladeless carpenter's plane, wooden barrel staves, and even chain mail, that it is very easy to imagine a Norse ship wintering there.

AN INTERCONTINENTAL TRADE NETWORK

The arrival of European goods everywhere quickened the pace of trade, long before the coming of Europeans themselves. In the Western Arctic, particularly, an immense all-Native trade network centred on Bering Strait grew up, one that eventually encompassed even the Copper Inuit. As we have seen, Asian iron was available in small quantities from very early times. Then in the seventeenth century, the Russians began pushing east across Siberia. In 1649 they established a small trading post at the mouth of the Anadyr River in eastern Siberia. Soon goods from this post were making their way into Alaska, and in much greater quantities than before.

The pace quickened again in 1788, when the Russians signed a peace treaty with the Chukchi of far northeastern Siberia, and the following year opened a trading post at the mouth of the Kolyma River specifically aimed at the Bering Strait trade. What the Russians wanted were furs, and what they offered in exchange were mainly iron goods and, later, tobacco. An annual trade fair at the post attracted a growing body of professional Native middlemen, mainly Chukchi, but also Alaskan Inuit. They took Russian trade goods purchased at the post to Inuit trade fairs held at Cape Prince of Wales on Bering Strait, and at nearby Kotzebue, where they were exchanged for a considerable mark-up, along with other more local trade goods such as ivory, wooden artifacts, and spotted reindeer hides.

From here distribution networks fanned out to more distant trading centres. The most northeasterly trading centre in Alaska was located at Barter Island, near the present Canadian border. Here Alaskan Inuit traders were met by Mackenzie Inuit coming west from Herschel Island and the large beluga-hunting villages near the mouth of the Mackenzie River. A brisk trade was carried out every year, with Russian iron goods as a staple, along with animal products such as hides, furs, and sacks of blubber. In 1789, the same year the Kolyma post opened, Alexander Mackenzie visited the Mackenzie Delta and reported that Russian iron was already available there. It must have just become so, for thirty-seven years later Mackenzie Inuit told the explorer John Franklin that trade with Alaskans had begun within their own lifetimes.

By the 1840s this network appears to have expanded east again to include the Copper Inuit, whose contribution seems to have consisted almost solely of soapstone lamps and pots. Soapstone is not available in the Western Arctic, where people had always made vessels from pottery or various other rocks like schist. Soapstone is a far superior material, however, and when it became available was quickly substituted. Alaskan Inuit believed that soapstone lamps miraculously burned less oil than those made of other substances.

Lamps and pots were traded already finished because of their weight. Manufactured mostly at Tree River on the southern coast of Coronation Gulf, where there was a

Western Arctic Inuit smoked an aboriginal style of pipe based ultimately on Chinese opium pipes.

The split glass bead that ornaments this Alaskan labret was traded across Bering Strait from Siberia, and perhaps ultimately from China or Korea.

The blade of this harpoon head is made of European iron. Copper Inuit were receiving Hudson's Bay Company iron from Chipewyan Indian traders as early as the 18th century.

Inuit, in exchange (we are told from traditional accounts) for Russian iron knives. Two trade routes existed. One led across southern Victoria Island to Nelson Head on the southern tip of Banks Island, then over the winter ice to Cape Bathurst. The other, probably more important, route led straight west across the Arctic coast. The Copper Inuit became known as far away as western Alaska as "the people who make stone lamps."

ON THE EVE OF GREAT CHANGES

For a brief period, the Copper Inuit were the outer terminus of this intercontinental all-Native trade network. Within a generation it was gone. In the 1850s the Hudson's Bay Company began direct trade with Inuit in the Mackenzie area, and the American whaling fleet out of San Francisco was opening up trade in north Alaska. Both could supply metal knives, pots, and iron lamps far more cheaply than Inuit middlemen, and the entire network went into a

rapid decline.

Fortunately, perhaps, the Copper Inuit had other access routes to the outside world. One of the most important was through the Caribou Inuit living inland from the west coast of Hudson Bay. In the eighteenth century the Hudson's Bay Company established a post at Fort Prince of Wales, the site of present-day Churchill, Manitoba. All through the nineteenth century the Caribou Inuit traded with this post, exchanging furs and musk-ox hides for the usual metal goods. From an early date they also seem to have been trading with Copper Inuit, apparently acting as middlemen, taking Copper Inuit furs and hides and exchanging them at a considerable mark-up for Hudson's Bay Company trade goods. Tattannaaeuk, a Caribou Inuit interpreter on the first Franklin expedition, reported in 1819 that such a trade had already begun with Arctic coast people. It continued until 1916, when the first trading posts were established among the Copper Inuit.

The Copper Inuit met their Caribou Inuit trading partners at a rendezvous called Akilinik on the Thelon River, travelling southeast through Bathurst Inlet. It was customary for people to go down in

spring and return in autumn when there was enough snow cover for sledding. Sometimes Caribou Inuit made the trip in reverse, more out of curiosity and friendliness than for any other motive. They used a brief formula or song to describe their Copper Inuit friends: "They are good people to meet, they are pleasant companions. They always have plenty of seal meat. They are a friendly people. Whenever they go sealing they always secure plenty of seals."

A final source of exotic materials before the fur-trade era was a British Navy ship, HMS *Investigator*, abandoned off the northern end of Banks Island in 1853. It was soon found by wandering

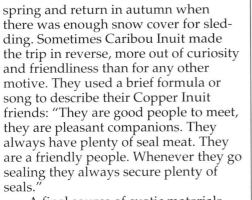

Kanghiryuarmiut hunters from Victoria Island and systematically scavenged for nearly forty years. The captain, Robert M'Clure, had left a depot on shore that was a particular target even after the ship itself sank (or was crushed by ice).

Not surprisingly, the Inuit were particularly interested in the metal: iron nails, barrel hoops, and the like. Softwood was also taken, but the hardwood fabric of the ship and the oak barrel staves were not of much use. Inuit informants remembered that hardwood, of which they had had no previous experience, was almost as difficult to work as antler but not nearly as strong. Material from the ship seems to have been traded widely among the Copper Inuit, in the days just before they were engulfed by the outside world.

ILLUSTRATION CREDITS

PHOTOGRAPHS
All objects illustrated in this work are from the collections of the Canadian Museum of Civilization, and were photographed by Stephan Poulin/Mia and Klaus, except the following:

Fred Bruemmer: pages 64, 65, 66 lower, 67, 72 lower, 106, 107, 110, 111, 123, 134, 135

George Calef/Masterfile: pages 108, 109

Wayne Lynch: page 66

Guy Mary-Rousselière, O.M.I. © Education Development Center, Inc.: pages 9, 12-13 lower, 16 lower left, 17, 25, 28-29, 30-31, 32-33, 36 lower, 51, 54-55, 57, 59, 60, 61, 69, 74-75, 83, 86, 88-89, 97, 100-101, 113, 116, 117, 119, 120-121, 132 lower, 133 lower, 139, 142-143, 144-145, 146, 147, 148, 149, 151 lower, 152, 153 upper, 156-157

Mia and Klaus: pages 20-21, 22, 23, 73

Canadian Museum of Civilization: R.M. Anderson: pages 68, 70-71, 84, 99, 114-115, 141; Harry Foster: pages 14-15 lower, 39, 62-63 lower, 94 upper, 95, 104, 126; Diamond Jenness: pages 24, 52-53, 98; J.J. O'Neill: pages 112, 140; V. Stefánsson: page 115 upper; G.H. Wilkins: pages 8, 10-11, 27 upper, 82

Stephan Poulin: page 6

Queen's University Archives, Chesterfield Collection: pages 26-27, 50, 85, 96, 138

Superstock/John Warden: page 21

ORIGINAL ILLUSTRATIONS
Frédéric Back: page 13, 14, 18, 22, 34, 35, 37, 41, 42, 43, 44, 45, 46, 47, 48, 49, 62, 64, 65, 72, 73, 74, 76-77, 80-81, 87, 118-119, 126-127, 130, 131, 136, 137, 144, 150

MAPS
Mountain High Maps, Digital Wisdom Inc, Jean-Luc Bonin: pages 39, 43, 44, 47, 48

SELECTED BIBLIOGRAPHY

Balikci, Asen. 1970. *The Netsilik Eskimo*. Garden City, N.Y.: The Natural History Press.

Damas, David, ed. 1984. *Arctic*. Vol. 5 of *Handbook of North American Indians*. Washington: Smithsonian Institution Press.

Hall, Judy, Jill Oakes, and Sally Qimmiu'naaq Webster. 1994. *Sanatujut: Pride in Women's Work*. Hull: Canadian Museum of Civilization.

Hansen, Jens, Jorgen Meldgaard, and Jorgen Nordquist, eds. 1991. *The Greenland Mummies*. Montreal and Kingston: McGill-Queen's University Press.

Harrington, Richard. 1981. *The Inuit: Life As It Was*. Edmonton: Hurtig.

Jenness, Diamond. 1922. *The Life of the Copper Eskimos*. Vol. 12 of Report of the Canadian Arctic Expedition, 1913-18.

Jenness, Diamond. 1928. *People of the Twilight*. Toronto: Macmillan.

Jenness, Diamond. 1946. *Material Culture of the Copper Eskimos*. Vol. 16 of Report of the Canadian Arctic Expedition, 1913-18.

Jenness, Stuart, ed. *Arctic Odyssey: The Diary of Diamond Jenness, 1913-16*. Hull: Canadian Museum of Civilization.

Maxwell, Moreau. 1985. *Prehistory of the Eastern Arctic*. Orlando, Fla: Academic Press.

McGhee, Robert. 1978. *Canadian Arctic Prehistory*. Toronto: Van Nostrand, Reinhold.

McGhee, Robert. 1994. Disease and the Development of Inuit Culture. *Current Anthropology* 35: 565-93.

Michea, Jean. 1967. *Esquimaux et Indiens du Grand Nord*. Paris: Société Continentale d'Éditions modernes illustrées.

Morrison, David. 1983. *Thule Culture in Western Coronation Gulf, N.W.T.* Mercury Series Paper 116. Archaeological Survey of Canada. Ottawa: National Museum of Man.

Morrison, David. 1992. *Arctic Hunters: The Inuit and Diamond Jenness*. Hull: Canadian Museum of Civilization.

Murdoch, John. [1892] 1988. *Ethnological Results of the Point Barrow Expedition*. Washington: Smithsonian Institution Press.

Rasmussen, Knud. 1931. *The Netsilik Eskimos: Social Life and Spiritual Culture*. Vol. 5 of Report of the Fifth Thule Expedition, 1921-24.

Rasmussen, Knud. 1932. *Intellectual Culture of the Copper Eskimos*. Vol. 9 of Report of the Fifth Thule Expedition, 1921-24.

Taylor, William E. Jr. 1965. The Fragments of Eskimo Prehistory. *The Beaver* (spring): 4-17.

NOTE: The quotation appearing on the *frontispiece* (page 7) is taken from Knud Rasmussen's *The Netsilik Eskimos,* pg. 379.

Printed in Spain